GRAND SLAM

I

ELIN

a'm teulu

yn enwedig

DYLAN, LWL a MEG

GRAND SLAM

Editor: John Hefin

Y Lolfa

First impression: 2007

© John Hefin, the contributors and Y Lolfa Cyf., 2007

Cover and typesetting: Dafydd Saer

ISBN: 978 184771 017 8

Printed, published and bound in Wales by
Y Lolfa Cyf., Talybont, Ceredigion SY24 5AP
e-mail ylolfa@ylolfa.com
website www.ylolfa.com
tel 01970 832 304
fax 832 782

Er cof am

R A Y

(1951–2007)

Contents

Ray Gravell

Introduction

The late, great Scarlets, British and Irish Lions Coach, Carwyn James always maintained that rugby football was a "thinking man's game". The poet Dic Jones wrote of him, 'His world was Welsh, his Wales worldwide.'

Carwyn was most certainly a visionary, and way ahead of his time. These attributes and qualities also belong to a very dear friend of mine and Carwyn's – John Hefin, the former Head of Drama at BBC Wales. John, like me, was deeply influenced by our mutual friend, Carwyn had coached John as a young boy at Ysgol Llangynfelin in the village of Taliesin, near Aberystwyth.

Carwyn was doing his Teacher's Training at the time when John's father, the late Hugh John Evans, was Headmaster of the school (John's mother Megan, by the way, was herself an active stage actress in her locality); an idyllic setting and upbringing for a young and enthusiastic pupil to be coached in rugby as well as other noble pursuits, by a man who was to be acknowledged not only as a rugby genius, but as one of the most distinguished Welshmen of his generation. Carwyn's coaching and John's direction

bear strong similarity – quietly passionate with a huge regard for each individual talent. I was lucky enough to have experienced both.

John benefited immensely from those early days of master class tuition, and the Carwyn connection came to full fruition at a time when Welsh rugby experienced an extraordinary decade called, rightly so, the 'Golden Era'. The seventies produced three all conquering Grand Slam sides and I was indeed privileged, honoured and thank God lucky enough, to have been a playing member of the 1976 and 1978 teams. (Sadly I did not play in the Paris game which was central to the film because of an injury sustained in the second half of a game between Cardiff and Llanelli. I went to tackle one Gareth Edwards – got one of my shoulder nerves crushed, which kept me out for four months!)

John, himself a robust No. 8 in his day, was never capped and never played in a Grand Slam side, but as a film producer and director was a true 'International', as this film – acknowledged and revered by the viewing public and critics alike – proves. It is quite simply 'Epic'.

We had our rugby greats such as Mervyn Davies, Gareth Edwards, Gerald Davies, Phil Bennett and JJ Williams, to name but a few. The film had its greats in principal actors – Oscar winner, Hugh Griffith, Windsor Davies, Dewi 'Pws' Morris, Siôn Probert and BAFTA Cymru best actress Sharon Morgan. And there you have it, a rare and talented collection of players and performers who, each in their own inimitable way, contributed on turf and screen to a collective memory of a great era; a memory to this day that enriches and unifies our ancient nation.

This book means so much to me – the obvious pleasure of writing this foreword but more importantly it's involved the men and women who made the Grand Slams possible; men and women who possess a generosity of spirit which has been priceless during the last six months of my life. Their phone calls, letters and cards have offered solace beyond measure. If I may mention one, as a representative of the performers and players – Siôn Probert, writing as if he were Maldwyn. His weekly spiritual and wicked wishes have been a life force. *Diolch yn fawr* to you all.

Enjoy this book, which describes in vivid detail the creative process that made the film possible. It also clearly illustrates that there was as much laughter behind the camera as there was on screen. Now that's funny!

Ray Gravell

Llanelli, Carmarthen County, Irish Wolfhounds, Barbarians, Wales, British and Irish Lions President / Llywydd Llanelli Scarlets and of course Mynydd y Garreg RFC.

Gerald Davies

Reflections

I believe that Grand Slam is the funniest film ever about rugby.

I grew up thinking that the Ealing comedy *Run For Your Money* was a good shot at creating the atmosphere of the misadventures that can and did occur during what inevitably turns out to be a gawky and imperfect rugby weekend in London when Wales are due to play England at Twickenham. We followed the antics of Hugh Griffith, Meredith Edwards and Donald Houston as the hapless supporters. It also starred Alec Guinness and Joyce Grenfell, with the seductive Moira Lister adding the metropolitan glamour among the many gabardine overcoats.

Whether *Run For Your Money* has survived the passage of time I am not sure, but for me I find that *Grand Slam* certainly has. I find that I laugh still at the ill-fated adventures and the unfulfilled dreams of Mog, the two Lloyd-Evanses, and the camp hopes of Maldwyn Novello-Pughe as much now as I did when I first saw the film. This was when I had a sneak preview of the rough cut long before anyone else was to be exposed to its hilarity and sentiment.

I was privileged to see it in its embryonic state in a cutting room in the BBC studios in Llandaf. John Hefin and Gwenlyn Parry, the maestros who inspired the film, Chris Lawrence, the editor, along with the Falstaffian figure of Rhydderch Jones, invited Geraint Evans (John's brother) and myself to see it.

This was before Christmas 1977. Geraint and I decamped from the office mid-morning hoping to return by early afternoon before the annual Christmas party began. But we enjoyed ourselves so much – laugh-out-loud fun – at the BBC and talked about the film for so long afterwards that, loitering so enjoyably as we were, we were noticeable for our absence on our return to what was by then the in-full-swing office bash. The Executives were expected to be present, from the beginning. We were late. We were given a pretty serious dressing down from one of the higher-ups who doubtless on hearing our explanation, and the fantasy we had lived, was upset that this privilege had not been extended to him.

This was apparently when the film passed the test, as John later told me. Since he and Chris had lived with the film and its production for so long they were no longer able to have a genuine feel for what they had done. Was it any good? Geraint and I, so they said, had laughed not only at all the incidents and the affectionate and wildly idiosyncratic characters but also in unprepared for and unexpected places.

They were made to feel suddenly at ease.
The game was on. From Caradog Lloyd-Evans
in his funeral Homberg chasing his 'butterfly'
nostalgically around the Sacre Coeur, Glyn's vision
of a personal grand slam and Wil Posh's descent from
barely intelligible 'born-to-the-purple' accent into
gobbledygook and finally to impenetrable blubber are
studies of a rugby weekend's disappointments, hopes
and potential disintegration.

I laugh with and at them still. It is a classic.

Gerald Davies

Cydweli, Cardiff, London Welsh, Barbarians, Wales,
British and Irish Lions.

Maldwyn Novello-Pughe

Disclaimer

Maldwyn Novello-Pughe

Cwrt y Frenhines
Ocean View
Specific Ocean Pallisades
Malibu Beach
California

Yew knows me, Readers; I don't say much; but this I will say… (and they'll most likely edit it out knowin' them lot).

I hated every second of that apology for a film. I am tampin' with angst to this day. Siôn Probert was far too old to play me in the first place, (as Siôn's granddaughter, Bethan, will tell yew STRAIGHT).

Beein as 'ow I am a tax exile by 'ere in Hollywood (No! not Hollyhead); I am, as I writes, linin' up a sequel what will have much more originality, authenticity, Depth and Thrust, in order for to right the wrongs what have been done to my reputation irregardless of my nerves.

I still wakes up screemin' about it.

Brad Pit will be playin' me. From the sirname alone, 'sobvious he's a Rhondda boy, innit?

I'm nowjest coachin (No! not cwtchin) him by my pool and jackewsie on the appropriate accent and body langwitch to ewse as we listens to the sound of the waves in my sea-front, secluded 'arsienda.

Brad walks just the same as what I do, which is a 'ewge plus.

Catherine Zeta Jones is 'ammerin on my door day and night like a thing possessed – upsetting the servants in a vain attempt to secure the roll of Odette wot Sharon Morgan played – Topless! – the brazen courtizone!

Orlando Bloom (stark naked)… please forgive my wonky handwritin' … is veery keen to do Dewi Morris (in the nicest sense of the word) as Glyn.

I am toyin' with Kirk Douglas to play Hugh's role as Mr. Lloyd-Evans. Any other suggestions will be welcome.

I don't mind telling yew now that I am goin' spare by ere bein' BOMBARDED with constant continuous phone calls from Zsa Zsa Gabor, Elizabeth Taylor and Joan Collins beggin' to play Marika's madame. I've got my eye on Gina Lollobrigida… as long as her name can fit into the 'credits'.

Whatever the final outcome of my Star-Studded Epic sequel, the Make-up and Hairdressin' bills will go 'through the roof'. Serves them right an' all.

Windsor don' need no replacement as Mog

– he's very well equipped to perform again… and I means that in a 'nice' way. His wife Lynne is a martyr to his demands to this day (pity he's hooked on Viagra)… God 'elp too!!

There is one – and only one – more thing I wants to say; this concerns John Heavin 'Director' (note the perverted commas!).

A cat can have kittens in the oven but it don't make them Welsh cakes, do it?! He couldn't direct 'the Proverbial into a bucket!' I rests my case.

Oh!! Brad is shoutin' for me now from my sonia bath, so I'll have to cut this short, cos I don't want 'im getting steamed up for too long… not yet anyway.

'Elp my head! I'm feelin' a tremor from the San Andreas fault, but fair play it could be because Harrison Ford and George Cloony have plunged into my pool. It's not an hearthquake I'm 'appy to say.

WORRA RELIEF!!

Ever Internally Yewers,
Maldwyne. X.

(Coutewrier, Consultant to the Stars and the Coco Channel of Cimla.)

Must dash now to get my 'roots' touched up: I can't cope round 'ere unless I'm blonde.

M.N.-P. AC/DC AND BAR… ANY BAR.

John Hefin
Director

John checking details.

Fortuitous moments and the hindsight of 30 years lead me to believe that the first scene of this film neatly conveys the spirit of the hundreds of scenes that follow.

You may remember a council road sweeper in a yellow safety jacket, busily brushing a pavement somewhere in South Wales. He looks up and sees an oncoming hearse. In a spontaneous, fumbling manner, he stops working, removes his bobble cap and assumes a position of commiseration. Within the screen it all works.

The facts, however, are somewhat different, and I feel a little guilty as I recall that morning's shoot. The intention was to see the hearse, followed by a considerable cortege of black mourners' cars, snaking down a valley road. Sadly, however, there was no money for the considerable cortege – the hearse had swallowed most of what was laughingly called a budget, and, therefore, the opening scene was a bit on the thin side. I need not remind the reader that if the opening scene does not work, the TV zapper will soon decide matters.

Then I saw the yellow-jacketed sweeper, and – remembering that the hearse had to be returned to the undertaker's parlour that minute, as we had only hired it for an hour – in a flash of panic, I asked this bemused council employee (who was minding his own business, and who must have thought me odd, to say the least) to see in his mind's eye an imaginary hearse purring alongside his pavement, to stop brushing and, finally, to look sad.

Praise be! He did all three splendidly and I think he was paid a fiver on the spot – big money in 1976, for five minutes brushing and imagining.

And so, I hope you begin to see, that *Grand Slam* was shot on the hoof, was highly dependent on good will, and lived and died by certain guiding thoughts, one of which was: 'Chance comes best to the prepared mind' (Anon); another was: 'It is better to ask for forgiveness than permission' (Huw Wheldon). Also, somewhere in the background, Lloyd George's words echoed: 'Don't try, do it', and, if I'm not mistaken, Henry Ford's dictum: 'If you think you can, you can; if you think you can't, you're right,' made its presence felt throughout the whole production.

However, this is all recollection in tranquillity; at the time, we were quite simply busking, flying by the seat of our pants – but (and it was a big 'but') working to 'The Plan'. More of 'The Plan' later!

'To begin in the beginning', as the most famous Jack ever once said, Welsh rugby was simply superb in the 70s. Witness the record – three Grand Slams in one decade. That taste of excellent rugby was palpable and there to be savoured by one and all; that taste was to become a critical factor in our film.

D J Thomas, the assistant head of programmes in BBC Wales, made a suggestion (he would never issue an instruction) that the outline that Gwenlyn and I had submitted for production should be reconsidered, and placed within a rugby context.

Gwenlyn Parry, my great friend, who very sadly passed away on Guy Fawkes night, 1991, was one of Wales' leading Welsh-language playwrights. He was Head of Scripts at the BBC, and, as a collaborator, he was always displaying wit, originality and daring. William Gwenlyn Parry was from Deiniolen in Gwynedd; he had, among many other things, a

Gwenlyn Parry – friend, colleague and wit.

huge delight in brass bands, and the aforementioned outline featured the Deiniolen Brass Band in a road movie to Brussels. Great! But it was immediately scrapped, as we saw our boss's point. There was a hasty rewrite and a new outline submitted, this time with rugby players substituted for the brass band, in the shape of Caradog, Glyn, Mog, and a Trefor from North Wales.

Trefor was a rugby naïve, who had moved South, befriended rugby fanatics and was the butt of jokes, due to his ignorance of rugby. In many ways,

15

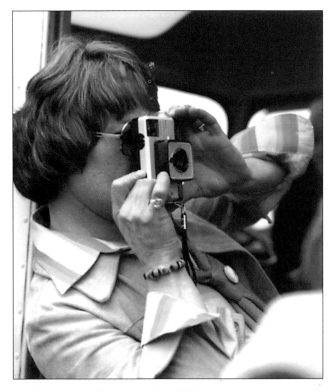

Maldwyn Novello-Pughe. 'Hold it.'

Trefor was Gwenlyn.

However, despite Trefor's appeal, a new character emerged during the shooting of another film I was directing, a few months prior to *Grand Slam*. It was *Mr Lollipop M. A.* by Rhydderch Jones – another good friend. This starred Charles Williams and Dame Flora Robson, and playing a small but significant part was one Siôn Probert. During the rehearsal breaks, Siôn would regale us with stories of Tarquin from Seven Sisters, who was known to say, "When I departed there were only six left." Tarquin was known in his community, not as a gay or as a homosexual, but as one 'who was good to his mother'. Siôn's characterisation and timing were immaculate and we were in 'non-PC' stitches during the rehearsal breaks; indeed, the breaks became lengthy and the rehearsals alarmingly short – but with actors like that, why worry too much? I introduced Siôn's humour to Gwenlyn, and overnight Trefor became Tarquin – or, to give him his stage name, Maldwyn Novello-Pughe, boutique owner (open late Tuesdays and Thursdays). *Grand Slam* was born.

Born, yes – but into intensive care. There were all sorts of pressures, e.g. the so-called budget was, as mentioned before, limited, and it was decided by middle management that Twickenham should replace Paris as a location; less travelling, much cheaper. We dug in our heels and won that one – it just would not have been the same without that *je ne sais quoi*, as Maldwyn would say. Again, due to a challenging budget, we only had a three-day shoot in Paris, and so all the foreign interior scenes (the strip club, hotel foyer, hotel bedroom etc) had to be shot in Cardiff – in 376 Newport Road, as it happens, the home of the BBC club. Why there? Because it was free of any facility fee and had a friendly steward.

Our next task was to cast and decide on a style of directing. I was both Producer and Director, which was a good thing, i.e. no passing the buck, except to myself, and I also had superb senior management on the third floor of Broadcasting House, Llandaf. By superb management I mean GSJ (HPW), which in everyday parlance, as opposed to 'BBC speak', was one Geraint Stanley Jones, Head of Programmes, Wales. Geraint was The Great Enabler, who knew his staff and was sensitive to their strengths and weaknesses. He eased our passage through the labyrinth of BBC bureaucracy, and became confidante and critic – not a bad combination.

I was determined to cast as many actors from Wales as possible. Indeed, all the Welsh and French parts, apart from the superb Marika Rivera (Odette's mother and the original Butterfly), were played by Welsh artists. Mici Plwm and Malcolm (Slim) Williams played Gendarmes, Elizabeth Morgan played the Parisian receptionist and of course Sharon Morgan played Odette.

Marika Rivera, who played the Madame and Odette's mother, was the daughter of the Brazilian ceramic artist Diego Rivera, and had been brought up in the company of Picasso and other luminaries in Paris. This colourful Russian-Mexican was a terrific force in the film. There is no such thing as a small part, only small actors. Well, she wasn't small, and filled the screen, and gave each of the nightclub scenes an authentic French ambiance. I have tried my best to trace her so that she could contribute to this book, but sadly to no avail.

Casting Maldwyn was a given – a stroke of luck. Casting Mog was also easy. Windsor was famous at the time for being the Sergeant Major in *It Ain't Half Hot Mum*, and therefore had a profile which would add immensely to the film's popularity. He was from

Marika Rivera, 'my little butterfly', with Hugh Griffith.

Mog, mid-ablutions.

Half-time… and it's going well.

Nant y Moel and knew rugby culture at grassroots level. Windsor was also a friend of Gwenlyn's as they had both been to the Normal College, Bangor. Casting the archetypal 'Hon. Sec.' was, therefore, easy, and, what's more, Windsor was a joy to work with. Another actor who is always a joy to work with is Dewi Pws Morris, a unique character; Mr Originality, who can get away with absolute murder. Dewi can tell the filthiest joke in a Vicar's tea party and, without fail, reduce the company to uncontrollable, rapturous laughter, without offence. Not many actors could have got away with his opening scene, as Glyn in the film, driving his father's hearse, wearing red racing gloves (Dewi's idea), blowing lewd kisses at Maldwyn and revving away with a 'V' sign.

Now Hugh Griffith. Getting him on board seemed to be a pretty high hurdle, at the time. Gwenlyn and I had decided that the best plan was attack, and, armed with a flimsy treatment of a film and an expensive bottle of brandy, we got on the 125 train to Paddington and taxied to his flat. True to say, we had fortified ourselves a little in the train's bar, as meeting the Oscar winner was a daunting prospect. We rang the bell of the apartment. Gunda, his German wife, answered and kindly led us into the lounge and there, as if on a throne, he sat. Greetings were exchanged (*yn Gymraeg*) and although we felt a bit like Greeks bearing gifts, the bottle of good Armagnac was proffered and much appreciated. So far so good. We talked of Wales, Anglesey, the RSC,

Lost in France, en route to the Bistro Paradis.

and Hollywood and, eventually, got to the purpose of our visit.

During this three-way conversation, which involved quite a lot of smoking and drinking, I noticed some of the details in the room: books, watercolours, cartoons, theatrical bric-a-brac, and on the table alongside his wing chair was the Oscar he'd won for *Ben Hur*. That was interesting enough, but what he did with it was even more interesting. Every time he had a cigarette, he put it in his mouth, reached for a match with his right hand, and held the Oscar in his left. (As you know, the Statuette is a naked man, with a broad sword held in front of him, doing the duty of a fig leaf on classical statues.) He would take the match to the Oscar and strike it, excuse my French, up its arse. Well, what else do you do with an Oscar? Just look at it? After each light-up, the conversation continued as if nothing out of the usual had occurred, and, indeed, much to our relief, by the end of one of the most memorable meetings of my life, Hugh (it wasn't Mr Griffith by now) had said, "Yes." Boy! Were we over the moon, leaving Paddington that evening!

Welsh actors are extraordinary (for an excellent analysis of that statement, please read Peter Stead's book, *Acting Wales*). They are, at best, inventive and brave, a bit like our best rugby players, and in the right environment are capable of magic. But how do you mine that magic?

With the aforementioned Plan. The usual rehearsal pattern for a TV drama involves a complete script (probably a fourth or fifth draft), plotting detailed moves and refining performances, in large draughty halls. We decided to do away with all that. This was a dangerous move as this conventional method was well tried and tested and certainly fitted in with the established BBC way of doing things. Everyone knows where they are; the shape of the production grows slowly, and can be witnessed by wardrobe, make-up and design, etc., during specific runs that are set up for their needs. We replaced that traditional pattern with the total approval of the cast by simply sitting down for ten days in a small, non-draughty hall, various bars and lounges etc., where we discussed the behaviour of the four characters. We imagined at length what each character would do in any given situation, and without going into detail, it is true to say that, by the end of the

Rock-steady Russ.

rehearsal period, the four had familiarised themselves with Glyn, Caradog, Mog and Maldwyn to the point of intimacy. Indeed, it could be said that if any of them had been woken up in the middle of the night they could, with the right cue, react in character.

Dewi and Siôn were extraordinary catalysts: they were fast; their acerbic wit and command of South Walian English was spot-on, and, therefore, the improvisation that occurred between them was of the highest order, it smacked of authenticity – the very stuff of good dialogue. Many of the lines that occurred in rehearsal were noted and used, but most of the lines that were included in the final edited film were spontaneous, and created by the actors on location.

We all felt ready to go, as Mog would say, "over the top."

"Not on," said some of the middle management of the BBC. "This is not the BBC's way of doing things."

"Where is the script?"

"Where is the complete breakdown of…" and so forth. I tried my best to placate matters but without much success. And as we went 'over the top', there were suspicions that we'd overstepped the mark, and I must confess to one or two nightmares which trod that line of thought.

As a matter of fact, when it came to the shoot, the crew coped with the shock of the new with élan, and the days in Paris and Cardiff flew by at an astonishing speed. It was an absolute pleasure, seeing our days of preparation bearing fruit. Somewhere along the line we'd mined some magic. 'The Plan' had worked.

Most of the time, the camera was hand-held, i.e. there was hardly any use of a tripod. Russ Walker, a kind, honourable Scot, risked his redoubtable reputation by agreeing to 'mount' the camera, as it were, on his right shoulder, thus achieving a documentary/news feel to the reportage. The final result of his work was rock-steady and eminently usable, and I shall always be grateful to him for having the confidence to try this largely untried method, as far as drama was concerned in the late 70s.

I cannot write a word further about this film without introducing one of its great unseen heroines. Her name: Beth Price, from Cwmgiedd. Beth and I had worked together for fifteen years, she was

John with Beth: thinking like the Pontypool front row, 'We may go up, we may go down, but we never go back.'

my PA and boss, I was her director and boss. We read each others minds. I wouldn't say, "I think we should book that hearse/bus/ aeroplane/whippet," without her answering, "It's done." She was a star and contributed in a remarkable way to the smooth running of what could have been a complete shambles.

She understood things that do not appear in any manuals on 'How to be a Production Assistant'. She knew the nature of the human spirit across all continents.

I well remember her in Rorke's Drift, South Africa, surrounded by hundreds of hungry six-foot-six Zulus. We were making a documentary, with the late Kenneth Griffith, on that famous incident in the Boer War (where, according to Stanley Baker, 13 VCs were won by Welshmen, to the accompaniment of Ivor Emanuel). We were in a remote location and into overtime; the Zulus were becoming impatient, not being used to filming, with all its hanging around waiting for the right conditions. Tempers were frayed, and there were still many scenes to be shot. Things looked nasty, but, thanks to Beth, the situation was saved. Somehow, she had acquired a mountain of loaves and she got us all cutting and filling sandwiches. These she delivered to the Zulus as if serving the local WI. Peace and sanity were preserved, and we got our footage. They say that one picture is equal to a thousand words; in this instance, one sandwich was equal to a thousand words of directing.

In that seventies decade, Beth and I made *Grand Slam* for BBC 1; nine hours of *Lloyd George* for BBC 2; we started *Pobol y Cwm* for BBC Wales, as well as a host of single plays … together. Three cheers for Cwmgiedd's answer to all Thinking Blond Bombshells.

The most accurate name for the professional cutter/film editor is 'Chef du Montage', and there is

none better than Chris Lawrence, my friend who cut *Grand Slam* (see the bearded one above).

He, we, I; cohabited together blissfully for six weeks, in a small darkened room off Newport Road, Cardiff. Then BBC premises, now an Irish bank. Maybe the Irish – with native cunning – sniff out areas of outstanding good vibes. The small room was constantly filled with thick clouds of tobacco smoke, the walls well-adorned with nubile beauties, tastefully undressed, and there were very few visitors. The uninvited were glared out with looks that could kill. Nevertheless, very special invitations were sent, for example, to my brother and his friend, Gerald Davies. They came, they laughed, and we knew there was a chance of success. Only a chance, but their natural (as opposed to kind) laughter injected confidence at a time when that commodity was at a low ebb. One had seen every laugh ad nauseam and every weakness, real and imagined, wreaked havoc on our sleep patterns. So a mighty '*Diolch*' to those two.

As a director, all you do – physically speaking – in the cutting room, is sit. This is in sharp contrast to the Pre-Production (casting, planning meetings, location finding, etc.), and Production (the actual shoot). Post-Production is absolutely static, apart from wanderings to the WC. At this stage, at best, you don't work hard, you think hard. It's a time when you achieve – or don't achieve – what you planned all those months, maybe years, ago. The exciting bit is that you can achieve things that you never dreamt of, if you've shot the right material and if you're in the company of a kind but firm kindred spirit, i.e. Chris.

Being of the 60s (we're both the same age), that liberating decade influenced us deeply. We relished risk and innovation, and, what's more, we were encouraged to do so by our boss, Geraint Stanley Jones. Not a bad milieu, as they say in the Mumbles, to work in.

I love Extras. I've liked them since well before Jack Rosenthal and Ricky Gervais heightened their roles with such brilliance. Peripheral human furniture – yes, but much more, and not necessarily on screen.

They are, in one sense, nearer to the crew than the cast. The *craic* during bacon buttie breaks, the one liner prior to a take, and the wink when things are going haywire always make life much easier for me. I tended to ask for the same ones from film to film, so as casts changed they remained constant; they became a sort of SAS in the midst of major players and their intelligence reports were hilarious. The hanky panky, the stroppy male lead, and the Diva behaviour of some 'stars' were vividly described. My lot were never malicious, but their privileged inside-view of events on their side of the camera was always a valuable, harmless distraction. They had, in my view, earned the honour of being gainfully indolent. They never get a credit on screen, so, thirty years late, here they are:

Walk on 2's: (They are often superb actors and may say a few lines) Haydn Edwards, Ernest Evans, Glyn Wheldon, Anne Price, Clive Gilvear, Allan Chuntz (also fight arranger and Charles Aznavour look-alike), Lowri Buckingham, Marie Claire, Mici Plwm, Terry Denton, Tony Miles.

Walk on 1's (As *Walk on 2's* but don't have lines and may only react as a crowd): Bob Watson, Vince West, Mark Annandale, Gary Twomey, Bernard Plant, Ken Gardner, Ted Wyman, Djon Hampton, John Cadwalladr, Martin Griffiths, Tudor Walters, John Cassidy, John Corway, Lloyd Winters, Jack Sholimar, C Gee.

Extras: Dai Davies, Arthur Jones, Bob Gower, Neville Ackerman, Thelma Corway.

The Extras with Dillwyn Owen – Will Posh, bottom right.

Wynne Jones, the First Assistant

Many things occurred during the making of *Grand Slam* that are unprintable and unrepeatable. After all, what happens on tour stays on tour! Of the repeatable here are some examples.

• Imagine the set of a strip club, which is supposed to be in Paris but is, in fact, in Newport Road, Cardiff – at nine in the morning: "Romantic beyond," (as Maldwyn would say). We'd had our bacon butties and everybody was ready to roll. The late Wynne Jones, the First Assistant, was in charge of the strip club set. He was ably assisted by Dic Williams. Wynne ran every show he worked on with military efficiency. He'd 'done' studios galore, test matches, internationals, cathedrals – but never a strip club.

The scene involved Maldwyn telling the tale of a domestic problemette. As I recall, he'd told it the night before, to the crew and the cast, over a Babycham cocktail. The joke was so good that it was immediately commandeered for inclusion in the scene. Now, it's one thing to tell a story in a bar late at night, quite another to retell it at nine in the morning to people who already know the punch line. The joke goes something like this:

Maldwyn sits by a stranger, a bearded Frenchman, who does not understand a word of English.

Maldwyn:

You reminds me of someone – 'ang about, I'll put my finger on it in a minute … ah! That's right, Denzil, Auntie Gwennie's husband!

More 'fun fur', and lager…
whilst discussing Stanislavski.

Denzil … you know, you're the spit of him. (He confides and lowers his voice.) She 'ad terrible trouble with that man! I met her down the wool shop a few weeks ago. She was peaky – peaky isn't the word, love! She was ashen. I said, "Auntie Gwennie, what's the matter?"

"It's Denzil," she said. "He's been retired from work three months now, and he's under my feet all day and all he can think about is … sex … you know, the other." (As an aside) She's complaining; she should be so lucky! Anyway, she said, "My home is in a terrible state with him, I can't do my working surfaces, I can't clean anything, low dusting is out of the question, when he's at it all the time. I'll tell you how bad it's got: last Friday – no, I tell a lie, it was last Thursday – half past ten, five and twenty to eleven, I went to the deep freeze to get a chicken and he leapt at me there and then."

Well, I said, "Don't worry about it, it's just a little domestic upset."

"Domestic, nothing!" she said. "I was in the middle of bleedin' Tesco!"

We had three takes. Why? Russ, our cameraman, could not keep his camera steady. Why? Because he could not stop laughing! He'd tried stuffing his mouth with a handkerchief, putting plugs in his ears, but to no avail, until take three. He confessed later, much later, that he'd shut his eyes during the entire take and thought about really awful tragedies, so as to divert his attention. Without that genuine reaction from Russ, how much more difficult it would have been for Maldwyn to tell, let alone repeat, an old joke. It was, as they say, a bonding moment.

A few days into the shooting schedule, certain patterns emerged, e.g. corpsing during (as above) or after the take. The ad-libbing meant that each funny line or look was heard for the first time on camera – live, as it were. Consequently, every time I said, "Cut!" the actors involved (as well as the rest of us) collapsed in mirth. Only once or twice (honestly), I could not resist delaying saying "Cut!" for a few very long seconds, to see the look of apoplexy that comes when you've just got to keep a straight face, at the same time as wanting to burst out laughing. However, they soon rumbled me and sought revenge!

Odette and Glyn waiting for 'action'.

• Later that day, we did what was affectionately known as 'The Bonking Scene', a much-awaited scene involving Sharon and Dewi in bed. I felt it wise to make it a closed set and this made it far more comfortable for both actors.

Alan Taylor's bedroom set had a chic Parisian feel about it (I felt reassured that he'd researched such a set many times!). He was assisted by Gerald Murphy as well as the prop buyer Gwenda Griffith: this was her first job in television. Today, she's one of television's best producers in both Welsh and English. She was, and is, the ultimate stylist. Alan and I had been friends and colleagues for many years. He was the first designer I had ever worked with: lucky me, as he was inspirational, and taught me much about art and design, being a consummate artist himself.

The nervousness surrounding this bedroom set was – how shall I put it – charged. It was difficult and a little embarrassing to get it started, but after a few hesitations, both Dewi and Sharon were in bed naked – well, not quite naked; according to Dewi, Sharon had kept her socks on. Sharon and I had discussed this difficult scene many weeks prior to this moment, and, naturally, as a woman, she wanted to look good, and not in any way to look common. This, therefore, had to be a moment of trust. A moment which required this trust was when she left Dewi in bed, and instead of draping herself in a convenient sheet, she would sit up topless, and walk across the room. The 'sheet draping' struck us as pandering to the viewers' suspect moral code, a sort of old Hollywood Hayes Law,

where lovers were only allowed in bed if they kept one foot firmly on the bedroom floor. It seemed to us that, having spent the night together, Odette and Glyn would hardly need sheets for modesty's sake. We agreed to shoot it as planned, but to postpone the decision as to its use until we viewed it together in the editing stage. Brave Sharon, she took a risk and did it in the seventies, mind you, with panache.

During the two to three hours we spent doing 'The Bonking Scene' (I know it only lasted a few minutes but you have to get it right), things became more relaxed. Dewi did fine work in helping Sharon to relax by telling her a string of racy jokes while we were adjusting lights and so on, but, unbeknown to them, their microphones were still 'live' and Mansel Davies, our sound recordist, could hear every line of their jokes. For some reason, Mansel (an ex-paratrooper and experienced sound recordist) had chosen to position himself and his recorder under the bed. When it came to the take, Mansel was still laughing at the jokes he was not supposed to have heard. He was also subject to the mattress's movements, i.e. up and down. Mansel was literally being semi-crushed by thrustful movements and echoes of jokes. This double action caused him, mid take, with tears of laughter in his eyes, to cry out, "Let me out of here, for God's sake, let me out!" He said later, when he'd recovered from his ordeal, that the experience was far worse than his first jump as a paratrooper.

• It was a Friday morning in Paris – the Friday

go. Maldwyn sat between Glyn and Mog in the back. Caradog sat in the front by the French taxi driver, Russ crouched near Glyn's feet and Mansel was, yet again, on the floor, this time by Mog's feet. They then all looked at me and slowly just shook their heads, conveying very graphically: "Full up, no room, goodbye!" with big smiles on their faces. So I retired gracefully with Gwenlyn and had a few quiet hours in the hotel, waiting for their return and reflecting wryly on what had happened.

The first thing to say is that the scene from Charles de Gaulle airport to the hotel ended up as a truly superb scene (see Russ's description on page 37). Within character, they responded naturally, and with great wit, to seeing various landmarks en route. It was improvisation at its very best. The incident reminded me of a momentous milestone in television history, when the first man stepped on the moon. Where was the nearest director? 238,863 miles away! A salient lesson.

•   It was late on a Thursday night; we'd just arrived in Paris and we'd done what we could in preparation for the crammed schedule ahead of us. After a magnificent meal in the Marais, Alan Taylor said to me, "Come for a drive around Paris." It was a beautiful spring night, still and moonlit. He was mad about cars and was a superb driver. I sort of hummed and ha'd as I felt I should be in bed fairly early so as to face the next few days.

"Come on," he said. "It'll do you good." And how right he was. Paris by day is okay, but Paris by night is something else, as I'm sure many of you

before the match, and it was going to be a long and busy day and night shoot. We'd got up early in the Hôtel Terminus, Gare du Nord, had breakfast together and discussed the day's shooting schedule.

The first scene to be shot involved a taxi taking the 'Fab Four' from the Charles De Gaulle airport to their hotel. We all seemed to know what to do, and all that was needed was to get into the taxi and

Siôn Probert, Windsor Davies, Cissian Rees (make-up), Colleen O'Brien (costume), Alan (dresser), Gwenlyn Parry, Beth Price, John Welch (lighting), and Mansel Davies (sound recordist) at the Parc des Princes.

Alan, the dresser, and Cissian Rees. Cast and crew in the background, including Janet Church, the make-up assistant, all with badges.

know. We were out for hours, taking in that elusive thing called *naws*, or mood – a 'thing' that is so important to any film. We talked endlessly of that often arrogant, always stylish city's contribution to mankind, and then, early in the morning, returned, utterly refreshed, to the hotel.

The mood of Paris was to be have been an important sub theme in the film. We had originally shot and edited a 75-minute film, which ended up as a 60-minute, due to the scheduling problems of Bill Cotton, Controller BBC1. Years later, to be fair, he did apologise for the cut, but I must say it was a cruel blow at the time. What disappeared on the cutting room floor were scenes of Maldwyn 'up those boulevards like a bat out of hell', Caradog absorbing some of the city's culture, and Glyn and Mog seated in one of those pavement cafés on the Champs Elysées, watching the world go by. It was all a little lyrical, and, in my view, it contained elements which would have added a further dimension to the visual impact of the film. That dimension, thankfully, lingers on in my memory, and Alan's night drive is an everlasting journey.

• The treatment Gwenlyn and I had prepared ended with Wales winning in Paris – what else did Wales do in the Seventies? That safe bet, of course, was lost on that shocking Saturday in Parc des Princes.

The kick off was at two thirty and we had turned up at eleven, with one camera crew and a second unit. The second camera was the responsibility of Ken McKay, another Scot, whose job it was to loiter with intent in and around the ground, looking for good, colourful, atmospheric shots, and this Ken did excellently. A second unit, whose brief is solely visual, can add immensely to the totality of any film.

We all wore badges, bearing boldly in French the fact that we were BBC staff and were to be allowed access to all parts of the Parc des Princes. I had instigated the wording and design of these badges, which were totally unofficial – it is better to ask forgiveness than permission. There was one little snag, though, in that my translation from English to French, duly proclaimed that we were BBC (so far so good) and then went on to say that we were *not* allowed access to the stadium. Thankfully, the ground officials read no further than the BBC bit, such were those halcyon days before security madness.

At around one o'clock, the team, our boys, came on to examine the pitch, dressed in casual clothes, not an advert in sight, not a whiff of sponsorship; Brains, Brawn, Rockport, Peter's Pies and the Plynlymon Sludge Company were to be distant additions to the game. Our heroes strolled confidently on the turf, giving it an occasional little kick, to test its nature. They talked to us as if taking a pre-match stroll on Cefneithin RFC pitch. They were cool before cool found its way into common usage. I do believe one or two of them had a quick fag before returning slowly to the changing room.

And then the tension mounted; this time, they ran onto the pitch in the red strip of Wales, their faces pictures of concentration. Whenever I see our team running onto the pitch, I get the same choking feeling. Oh, what I would have given to play for Wales!

Three National anthems were played, the Marseillaise (of course) then *Hen Wlad fy Nhadau* (of course) and then God save the Queen. Gwenlyn and I decided at that moment that we would capitalise on this anthemic matter and included some appropriate, somewhat political dialogue for Glyn during the bed

Glyn and Odette after the anthem.

scene with Odette, whilst watching the game. How times change; the thought of what is now seen as the English National anthem being played at any Celtic or Gallic fixture would find short shrift.

Being with the crew on the touchline was a rare treat and privilege; I can't imagine such a privilege being given today to any film company, unless, of course, a fistful of dollars was exchanged. We shot and relished every move of the game, shooting far more than the usual 10 to 1 ratio.

"You'll nae have enough film left for the second

half if you keep on at this rate," warned Russ.

"Who cares?" thought I, when you are in a world class situation and hot, red blood is coursing through every part of your body. I wished the game to go on for ever, no matter what the final result would be. Well, not quite, and the result was pretty shattering; it took time to take it in, not only as a Welshman, but as a director. My God, I haven't got a climax to the film! The four principal characters had to achieve their individual Grand Slams, and these depended totally on a whim. What to do with our flights, booked for our return to Cardiff the following day?

I'll tell you what we did. Gwenlyn and I stayed up all night, attempting to revise crucial, closing scenes, whilst everybody else we knew in Paris drowned their sorrows in the overflowing foyer of the Hôtel Terminus. An answer came at the crack of dawn on Sunday – an unscheduled day and an answer which middle management would thoroughly disapprove of.

With severe hangovers, Mog and Maldwyn and the crew turned up very, very early at the Parc des Princes. No badges, no permission, official or otherwise; nothing except bold as brass cheek. We blagged our way in and, to the accompaniment of suspicious looks from the French ground staff, shot the scene of Mog and Maldwyn after the final whistle. We couldn't end the film on a low, and we had to remind the viewer, through Maldwyn and Mog's new dialogue (dreamt up a few hours earlier), that the fixture the following year was at home, at Cardiff Arms Park.

And there, one year later, we beat the 'froggie caci-pots'.

● One of the saddest moments was the departure of Hugh from Paris. During the brief time we had been there, his health became progressively worse. For some reason, he would not take his medication and, despite our sometimes rather lame, sometimes insistent protestations, his brandy intake remained somewhat high. It all came to a head and we had to call the doctor. He, of course, recognised his new patient and was in awe of the star of *Tom Jones*, *Start the Revolution Without Me*, and, of course, the Best Supporting Actor in *Ben Hur*. As I saw Hugh being treated by this kind doctor, I couldn't help reflecting on happier times, when he would tell a story against himself. The Anglesey boy was on the set of *Ben Hur*. The scene was the one of the famous chariot race, with Hugh dressed as a mighty Arab in charge of beautiful horses that were to take part in the event. Just before the take, Willy Wyler, the director, approached Hugh and said, "Huw, do you speak Arabic?" (Who's improvising now? Hollywood!) Hugh answered with magisterial certainty, "Yes! Yes!" and every strand of hair in his bushy eyebrows bristled with confidence.

"Okay," says Willy Wyler. "Lights! Standby! … Action!" Huw, in his own time, put his strong brown arms around two of the magnificent beasts' manes and whispered, as only a Bancroft Gold Medallist from the Royal College of Dramatic Art could,

Gren, like Max Boyce, captured an age. His perceptive and loving cartoons in the Echo *epitomised the Valleys view of the world, the rugby view in particular. There was therefore no hesitation in inviting him to draw the opening and closing sequence.*

"*T'yd yma, cariad bach, i mi roi sws i ti!*"

"Cut!" says the pleased director, who again approached Hugh and said, "Jeez, Huw! I didn't know you spoke Arabic so well!"

This scene was a far cry from what I could see in front of me. I bent down and asked Huw, who was draped for some strange reason in Gwenlyn's long black leather coat, which made him look like a Gestapo reject, "What do you want me to do?"

"Take me home," he said, "to Wales," and this we duly did. An ambulance and a motorised wheelchair were quickly hired, thanks to Beth, and Hugh was accompanied to Charles de Gaulle Airport, to be flown home according to his wishes. The private medical company, which had arranged the ambulance and wheelchair, had also supplied a nurse; not just an ordinary nurse, but one who looked like Brigitte Bardot dressed in what can only be described as minimum medical – a macro skirt and tight white blouse. It did Hugh a power of good to be accompanied across the tarmacadam of Charles de Gaulle and to the steps of the plane by this goddess. Hugh, who was on oxygen, with plastic pipes everywhere, turned to the nurse just before embarking, patted her gently on her derriere and, in a most gentlemanly fashion, said, "*Diolch yn fawr, bach.*" She smiled, he returned home and, within all too short a time, Hugh had died.

It was the death of a gentleman and a great actor. For me, one of the tests of a gentleman is how he behaves drunk as well as sober, and we had ample

evidence of both during the shoot – Hugh passed with flying colours. As for the great actor, very little needs to be said. He was the Great Griffith, who left the world a happier and richer place, due to his extraordinary talent.

This book gave me the privileged opportunity to share my memories with the cast and crew; and so dear reader, with no more ado – let me introduce the first – Russ 'no-fuss' Walker.

Russ Walker

Cameraman

Before the filming started, John Hefin and I had a discussion about the camera technique we were going to use. It was decided that we were going to do as much handheld (*cinéma vérité*) camera work as possible. This was a problem as the cameras in those days were very heavy, not at all like the small digital cameras of today, and weren't designed to be put on your shoulder because of the balance and weight – if the cameraman wasn't built like an American football player, he would be in trouble. I had been to the 'Photokina' exhibition in Cologne and seen a new camera made by Arriflex; it was lighter, not by today's standards, but the balance was better. So we decided to hire one for the week's filming in Paris, with a set of new, fast lenses (distagons). Spending money on new and untried equipment was unusual and a big deal in those days, but John thought it would be worth it. Even now, when I watch *Grand Slam*, I can't believe how much cut film we managed to do in that short period in Paris.

Everything was a bit experimental on this shoot – whereas today we would use a Steadicam, to make

Clockwise from bottom left: air hostess Lowri Buckingham; chambermaid Marie Claire with Glyn; Maldwyn and supporters.

the pictures as steady as possible, we just bent our knees, held our breath and tried to glide over the ground. Since then, many programmes, like *NYPD* and *CSI*, go to great lengths to do the same sorts of things we did. Looking back, it was a trendsetter – the style of *cinéma vérité* was for the camera to just follow the actors, whatever they decided to do. There were no rehearsal moves for the camera or actors, which meant much more freedom for everyone and that was one of the reasons it worked. The actors were great; we all got on so well together – we were all too busy laughing to have time for temperaments or ego trips.

Unusually, one of the first scenes we did was one of the first scenes in the film. It was the scene in the hearse, with Dewi Pws driving and Hugh Griffith, the funeral director, in the front passenger seat. In the back of the hearse, where the coffin would have been, was myself with the camera, Mansel, on sound, with the microphone, the best boy (John Welsh) with the battery light, and John the Director. As you can imagine, there was not a lot of room left, in fact Oscar-winner Hugh Griffith had to put the clapper board on himself! With all the bodies in the hearse, it really did steam up the windows in the back, but from outside it looked like frosted glass. After a successful take, Dewi pulled the hearse over to the pavement, where a very attractive young mum happened to be pushing a pram. The poor girl got the shock of her life as Mansel wiped the window to see where we were. What the mum saw from the outside was a ghostly hand at the frosted glass in the back of the hearse!

When we went to Paris, we had to film all the airport scenes before we left, just to get the atmosphere, with supporters, the team and, of course, our own actors. It is a good job we did film as much as possible hand-held and with battery lights because with most of it we only got one chance. Of course, there were problems: for instance, I got a bad shadow on Dillwyn's back as he went upstairs, dropping beer cans at Rhoose Airport, but in the finished film it just looks like a shadow from one of the supporters. After finishing filming at the airport, we had to keep the crew and equipment to a minimum, so only Mansel on sound and myself on camera went on the flight; the rest of the crew and equipment went by road. The new camera had only two magazines of film, each only lasting ten minutes. This just about lasted for the flight, but, as we landed, I saw and managed to film Concorde out of our plane window. I got off the plane first so I could film everyone getting off. There was a bit of a panic as we got into customs – I had run out of film and I had to reload the film magazines in a black bag, like a mobile darkroom. In the middle of this manoeuvre, the Welsh team came through customs – I have never unloaded and reloaded so fast, and, mercifully, managed to get some great shots as they went through customs at Charles de Gaulle airport. However, after all that, the footage was never used in the film.

For a lot of us, the taxi trip from the airport to the hotel in Paris was the highlight of the film. On the first run, in the front seats we had the driver, myself with the camera, Mansel with tape-recorder and microphone, and a battery light was strapped to the window. In the back seat were Dewi, Siôn and Windsor. The ad-libbing from the actors was great, but near the end of the run, we were stopped by a Gendarme for having too many people in the car – but soon Dewi, Siôn and Windsor had him laughing as much as us. Needless to say, he let us off. Next run, we had Hugh Griffith and the driver in the front of the car and camera and sound in the back, with one of the actors to feed Hugh the lines. As we tried to make it look like we were all in the taxi at one time, we had to do one final run, with just the camera to pick up 'cut-aways' of a dog for the rabies story, a lady for Dewi, and an old woman for Huw. As there was no room for Gwenlyn or John, we played the sound back to them on our return – Gwenlyn was laughing so much, he just said, "I wish I could write stuff like that!"

When we got to the Hotel that first night, it was to find that the rest of the crew and equipment had not arrived. I waited until about 10.00 pm and then I phoned John Lanchester, the Film Unit Manager in Cardiff, to see if he had any news, only to be told not to worry, as Mansel was sensible and would be there soon. This was very reassuring as Mansel was standing next to me! The rest of the crew and equipment did, however, arrive at midnight, after a delayed road journey.

Next day, we filmed Hugh standing up in the taxi sunroof as if he was standing in a tank liberating Paris. As we were filming, unofficially, in and around the Arc de Triomphe, with all the traffic congestion, there was only one chance to get the shot.

Later, we filmed Windsor on his run from the jail to the rugby ground, again out of sequence as the match was not being played until the Saturday. The pace of our filming in Paris was incredibly fast, e.g. with the lighter camera and fast lenses, the shots on the Metro were all done on one short journey. It was all very well doing this filming at this fast speed, but we had no way of seeing what we had shot, as the film had to be sent from Paris to London to be processed and then on to Cardiff, so we couldn't see any of it until we got back.

And so to the day of the match! We got there very early, to film the atmosphere – lots of actuality shooting, bands getting off buses, pitch-marking, TV-rigging, fans arriving and so on. When it was time for me to go onto the actual playing pitch, someone tied my badge onto my lapel the wrong side up, so I just turned it over. John came up to give me last minute instructions and happened to turn my badge the wrong way again. I innocently turned it back, and he turned it the other way once again! At that point all became clear – I had to record the critical scenes of the film without the correct pass! So, I boldly walked in with the *Daily Telegraph* photographer, whom I knew, and who did have the right badge. When the players came out to inspect the pitch before the game, Gerald Davies and Gareth Edwards came over to speak with me, as I knew them from the 1968 British Lions Tour of South Africa, which I also filmed for the BBC.

After they spoke to me, no one seemed at all bothered with my being there; in fact,

Russ checking the Metro route with his new Arriflex camera.

when the cockerel was running on the pitch, and the Welsh supporter tried to tackle it, I just went on to the pitch and continued to get some great shots of all the players walking around and soaking up the atmosphere before the kick off. And this shot and eventual sequence, for me, captured perfectly rugby in Paris. I don't think I would have got away with this on any other of the home country grounds. When the teams ran out for the start of the game, I was getting great close-ups. In those days, match coverage was pretty static, so those touchline shots were very dramatic. However, I got the fright of my life when the president of the French Rugby Union caught me by the arm. I thought, this is it, I'm being thrown out, but fortunately he just pointed to the touchline, telling me not to cross it, as he had seen me on the pitch earlier.

We could only film for ten minutes at a time, as that was the length of each roll of film. My fellow Scott, Ken McKay, was doing second unit work up in one of the stands, with the heavy camera, getting spectacular wide angles. I well remember my assistant being very busy all afternoon, loading and reloading magazines for both Ken and myself.

Although all the filming of the match went really well, none of us were prepared for the result; it was unthinkable that Wales could lose. The most vivid memory I have after the game was when we all got together from our different parts of the ground to find that Maldwyn had been crying and all his mascara had run down his face – what a mess! I am still not sure if it was real, or down to the make-up department. That night was awful; we didn't know if the film would be scrapped, or if Gwenlyn and John could think up a new ending. Thankfully, they did, and on the Sunday we went off to Parc des Princes to film it. On arrival, we had another shock – the rugby stadium had been transformed into a soccer pitch, with nets, not posts. The only option left was to avoid the pitch and shoot the stands only, in wide angle, and then film the revised ending at Cardiff Arms Park, and make it look like Parc des Princes at a later date.

When we were back in Cardiff, we could at least see what we had filmed in Paris. It was reassuring to know it was okay, as in those days it was an occupational hazard, not knowing for certain what was on the film until it had been developed. There was no auto exposure or auto focus, and if you took your eye away from the viewfinder even the slightest pressure would result in fogging of film. Then there were reflections of microphones, film crew, or even myself, and mirrors, window panes or sides of cars to worry about. So different from today, when there is instant feedback on location. Thirty years ago, it could mean anything from one day, or, as in *Grand Slam*'s case, a *week* to worry if everything was alright.

Most of the interior filming was done in or around Cardiff, and the shots inside the plane were filmed at Rhoose Airport Museum, in a very old plane. We put a kind of greaseproof paper over the windows, to make it look like sky outside, and also to stop us seeing cars going past! The BBC club was used for the majority of the remaining interior scenes, such as the hotel foyer, Odette's bedroom, the French jail, the boys' bedroom and the nightclub.

Odette's bedroom scene was interesting from a lighting angle. The room was very small, but it did have a fire escape outside the window. I was able to put a five kilowatt tea light on it, shining through the window. This had two uses:

i)   It created a moonlight effect, and it lifted the overall light in the room; this was useful as the film stock was very slow and grainy in those days.

ii) It created that great sexy silhouette of Sharon on the wall.

The night club scene presented lots of chances to create atmosphere, using star filters, coloured gels on the lights, etc. The fight scene was allowed to run for a very long time, in one take, a credit to the actors and the camera being in the right place at the right time, so that the punches didn't look as though they were missing their target.

My favourite scene in the film was Huw's dream, when Dewi was dancing with Sharon. I took quite a risk by using a No. 5 fog filter. This diffusion effect was not what the filter was intended for but by combining it with a very strong ¾ back light and soft fill light I managed to get that soft halation on Sharon's beret, which was exactly the effect that I was trying to create.

Years later, I had to film the famous French flanker, Jean-Pierre Reeves, at his home in Toulouse, for a Carwyn James programme – he couldn't stop talking about *Grand Slam* and was so pleased to have been mentioned in it by Dewi and Siôn!

My overriding memory of this film was that it was a real fun film to work on – it was so hard not to shake the camera while I was laughing during sound takes that, at one stage, someone stuffed a handkerchief in my mouth. It was an epic experience, to be involved in *Grand Slam*, and the film I thought had no end is still going strong thirty years later.

FIN.

Russ Walker

Mog feels the pressure as Ernest Evans, supporter (far left), leads the appreciation.

Two friends from Coleg Normal, Bangor, discuss old times as Llwynhendy's answer to Sacha Distel looks on.

Not quite Paris, but good enough for Mog's boxer shorts.

Notice 'the ball'.

Window display at its finest.

Dewi Pws Morris

Glyn Lloyd-Evans

Some twenty years after *Grand Slam* was first shown on the BBC, a few of the original cast were invited to the Angel in Cardiff on the eve of the France v Wales match, to celebrate and to be interviewed by Sara Edwards about the success of the film. When questioned about my reactions, I replied that we hadn't realised, as a cast, that we were making such cults of ourselves. At least, that's what I think I said, and Sara was much too nice a lady to question my pronunciation.

My recollections of filming are very vague, due to fact that most of the actors were quite partial to a pint or two before, during and certainly after the day's shoot. I do remember, however, that we all had a lot of *fun* making *Grand Slam*, mainly because John Hefin encouraged us to ad lib whenever we felt the urge; so much so that every take would be different from the last. For example, if I recall correctly, the bonking scene went to 19 takes, and Sharon, beautiful Sharon, made things very hard for me at times.

What was nice about filming in France was that all the fans we met (including the boys in the Welsh team) were really enthusiastic about the whole thing and did everything they could to help.

The film, when it appeared, worked so well

that for the next few years I'd frequently get fans approaching me on the street, bemoaning their fate that, "My wife won't let me go to Paris again because of you bastards." The other inevitable question (invariably in two parts) was, "Hey, aren't you the bloke who was in bed with that French bird?" I'd pre-empt the second question with, "Yes, and before you ask, no I didn't, and even if I had I wouldn't tell you." They always smile that 'bet you did' smile, and walk away contented.

I remember turning up on the first day's shoot with my script unprofessionally stuffed into my back pocket. It was 7 o'clock in the morning and there, waiting in the middle of the set, was Mr Griffith (I never dared to call him Huw), stooped over a large, official-looking, attaché case made of the finest leather.

"Ah, there you are, you little w★★★★r." (Such was his term of endearment for little 'moi'.) Mind you, I was honoured – if he didn't like you he wouldn't call you anything; in fact, he wouldn't acknowledge that you were there at all.

"Come here, boy!" he said, and over I scuttled, under the impression that we were going to go over the first scene of the day and work in some improvisations, but no! Oh, no! He opened the hallowed leather case and lo! there in front of my amazed eyes was a full cocktail cabinet, complete with glasses, mixers and peanuts to boot.

"What are you having, boy?"

"Er, well, Mr Griffith, I don't usually drink alcohol this early in the morning." Storm clouds started brewing above the ferocious black eyebrows, so I quickly added, "But seeing as you asked, I'll have a large brandy." His eyes softened, grew wider and finally lit up like furnaces.

"I think we're going to get on all right, boy bach!" We did, thankfully, and for the next month I was as professional as a newt.

Mr Griffith didn't like rehearsing much. I could sense his aversion to it from the first day. "Look, let's stop pissing about and record the f★★★ing thing!"

John, having looked around at the rest of us, smiled and said, "Well, you heard what the man said, let's record the f★★★ing thing." And we did.

One evening in Paris, we went out to what I can only describe as an upper class strip club. There were groups of men in dinner jackets and ladies in expensive designer dresses, dining at tables laden with exotic food and the best champagne, and watching very beautiful, naked girls cavorting all around them. Mr Griffiths called it a 'tit and taters joint'. He was instantly recognised (it happened all the time in Paris) and was hustled onto the stage, to be introduced as 'Monsieur Ew Greeffeeth, actor internationalle, et grand celebrité' – or something like that. I wasn't really listening, being totally engrossed in studying the taters, or was it the tits? Cheers and applause all round for the man himself, and drinks all round on the house. Two hours later, we were all ceremoniously kicked out. The 'actor internationalle et grand celebrité' had pinched one of the strippers' bums and poured a pint over one of the bouncers

I suppose a… pint's out of the question?

Fantasies, fantasies...

What's French for 'Ref, are your parents married?'

– ah, well! *C'est la vie*!

He once told me that he believed that one day I would become a great actor and wit like himself, "Because you're only 22 now and you're a halfwit already." Goodnight, Mr Griffiths! Keep smiling down on us – I wonder if they do rehearsals in heaven?

When *Grand Slam* appeared on television, my mother was horrified. She being a chapel-going Methodist (but if you'd known my mam – one of the most fun loving jokey, irreverent Methodists in Wales). This film with rugby, drinking, bonking and nudity was the limit.

She really was ashamed of what I'd done and didn't go to chapel for a fortnight to avoid embarrassment. Fortunately the minister noticed her absence, and paid her a visit, asking why she had not attended for the last two weeks.

'It's that film, that *Grand Slam*, I'm so ashamed of our Dewi, he's let the whole of Treboeth down – I'll never hold my head up again.'

The minister smiled, looked Mam in the eyes and said, 'But it's one of the funniest things I've seen for years – you should be proud of Dewi – he played his part brilliantly'.

Next Sunday, Mam was in chapel, loudly enquiring to all and sundry, 'Did you see our Dewi in *Grand Slam*? Www! He's a terrible boy... but wasn't he good in it?!' She was proud as punch.

It's funny how religion can take over your life…

Dewi Pws

DEWI MORRIS

AS GLYN LLOYD-EVANS

B.A. ABER (FAILED)
BLINDSIDE FUMBLER

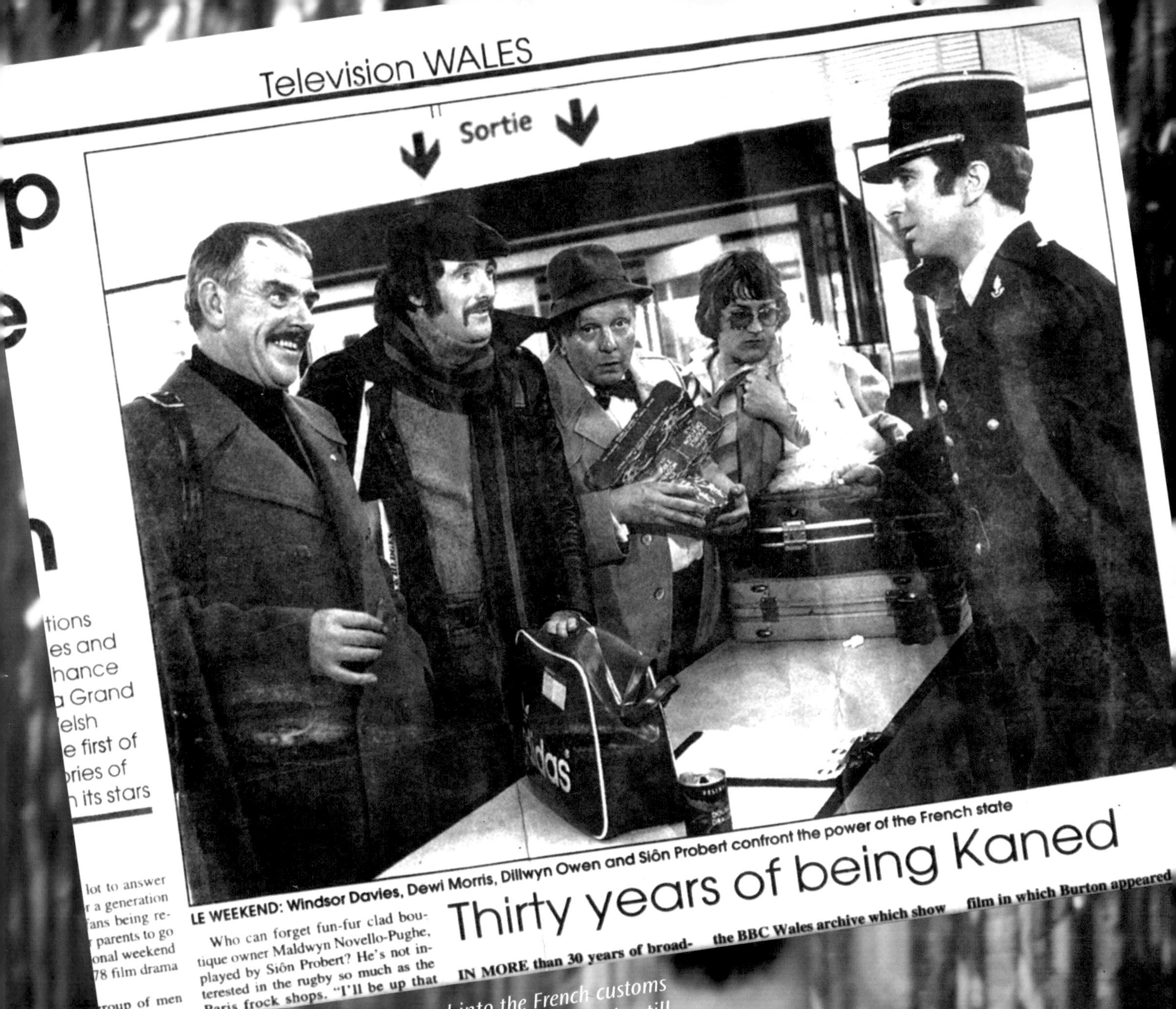

Television WALES

Sortie

LE WEEKEND: Windsor Davies, Dewi Morris, Dillwyn Owen and Siôn Probert confront the power of the French state

Thirty years of being Kaned

...tions
...es and
...hance
...a Grand
...elsh
...e first of
...ories of
...n its stars

...lot to answer
...r a generation
...fans being re-
... parents to go
...onal weekend
...78 film drama

...roup of men
...lleys as they

Who can forget fun-fur clad boutique owner Maldwyn Novello-Pughe, played by Siôn Probert? He's not interested in the rugby so much as the Paris frock shops. "I'll be up that

IN MORE than 30 years of broad-

the BBC Wales archive which show

film in which Burton appeared

BBC Llandaf, transformed into the French customs at Charles de Gaulle airport. Will Posh is still standing – but only just.

You should have played for Wales!

CULT CLASSIC: To coincide with Wales's Nations rugby finale against France, BBC Wales is screening a ge from its archives.
The comedy Grand Slam starring Windsor Davies, Sion Probert, Dewi Morris and Hugh Griffith, has enjoyed cult status since it was first screened in the late 1970s.
The play follows the fortunes of a group of Welsh rugby supporters on a trip to Paris to see Wales take on the French. The play is on BBC Wales tonight at 9.30pm.
This season's Wales against France clash is live on BBC2 Wales on Sunday , kicking off at 3pm.

FRIDAY, MARCH 17, 1978

''Grand Slam'', a play by Gwenlyn Parry on B.B.C., Friday, March 17, tells the hilarious story of the visit to Paris on Internationa Match day of a group of Welsh rugby supporters. Left to right: Maldwyn Pugh (played by Sion Probert), Mog Jones (Windso avies), Caradog Lloyd Evans (Hugh Griffiths) and Glyn Lloyd Evans (Dewi Morris) arriving in Paris.

Happy landings.

Elizabeth Morgan

Josephine, the French Concierge

Liz about to be goosed.

I'm not French at all. I'm Welsh from Llanelli, but I like to think I can sound pretty close, language-wise. John thought so, anyway; that's why he asked me to play the uncompromising lady with the booking ledger. I think he must have been stuck, because I remember having just a week's notice.

At the time, I was a member of the BBC Radio Drama Repertory Company in London and in the middle of a five-day rehearsal for a play directed by Ms Betty Davies, who had worked at BBC London for years, although her origins were in Aberystwyth. It was thanks to her that I was able to take a couple of days off from the studios.

The script of my scenes was sent immediately, but I use the term 'script' very loosely. It comprised a description of the set and the general shape of the scenes – a 'no room at the inn' scenario. The rest – i.e. all my French rabbiting – was left up to me to work out, and it had to be absolutely bang on – couldn't make any grammatical errors, especially as the film would be shown in La Belle France. So, having written my own dialogue and translated it into French, I hot-footed to a French chum, a teacher, who made a few tweaks, but mainly she listened to my accent.

All the way down to Cardiff, in the train from Paddington, I rehearsed my French lines – BBC Wales gave me a first class ticket for that very reason. There is infinitely more of a responsibility, when you are acting in another language.

It was great to meet up with all my old friends again. Through the years, Siôn and I have played every conceivable relationship on stage, radio and television, and Windsor and I had already played brother and sister in a long-running BBC TV series, 'One of the Family.'

In fluent French, Mog discusses the accomodation that Happy Valley International travel agents have organised – not.

I have to admit I was slightly disappointed that the location filming for me was to be Cardiff. The others were all going to Paris. And not even a swanky hotel in Cardiff, but the BBC club, Newport Road! As my Mum from Llanelli would have said, "They wanted their heads read!"

My raven wig in place, make-up done, we did one rehearsal, then John said, "Let's go for a take." It was during this take that Windsor sidled up behind the reception desk and pinched my derriere; the unforgettable 'goose'! This was NOT in the script. It was completely unrehearsed and if I looked gob-smacked – I truly was! We carried on to the end, thinking we would have to go again. But John loved it, and it was in the can. There was one other short scene at the reception desk, in which Windsor uttered his memorable ad lib in my direction, "Don't fight it, love!"

The laughter, the banter, the jokes, and the sheer

bonhomie of the short period of my involvement in *Grand Slam* remains a warm, smiling memory after all these years.

Nowadays, I spend most of my time in France, at my home in Vence, where I write books about France and articles for *French News*, an English newspaper published there. In fact, I shall be covering the France v Wales match in the Six Nations Tournament for the paper in March 2008. I'm a huge fan of Wales, but judging from their World Cup displays, I'll have a job on my hands. However, 'in Victory, magnanimity; in Defeat – DEFIANCE!'

There is a very special relationship between France and Wales. First of all, we have a common adversary, England, which features potently in international rugby. Once, chatting to a French village elder, who, when he knew I was Welsh and not English, told me of his many visits to the Arms Park to see France play Wales, and how he cried whenever he heard *Hen Wlad fy Nhadau*. He loved it!

The Draig Goch flutters flamboyantly from my French home and, a few years back, my rugby loving neighbours were nearly as deliriously happy as I when Pays de Galles won the 'Grand Schlem!' Then there's the strong linguistic tie with Brittany. More than that, Gaul was the area for Celtic settlements. Just 2 kilometres up the road is Tourrettes sur Loup, which was a thriving Celtic Ligurian town. No wonder I feel so at home.

And the people; I hate generalisations, but you can get as much *clecs* round here with the neighbours as I've ever heard dished up in Llanelli, and they drop in for a cuppa too, especially when I've got a batch of Welshcakes.

I can honestly say, if I hadn't been born Welsh, I'd have chosen French, so I shall be forever proud and very privileged to have been part of 'Grand Slam'.

Allez Pays de Galles! Allez France.

Elizabeth Morgan

Alan Chuntz, stunt arranger, who also stood in as a lookalike for Charles Aznavour.
'He's the talk of every tupperware party I've been to,' said Maldwyn.

A comfort break near Brackla.

Mansel Davies, sound recordist. Ex-paratrooper, who risked life and limb under a bed.

Alan Taylor
Designer

As I looked through the latest quarterly programme schedule, to enable me to assign programmes to various designers, I came across what I assumed was a sports programme entitled *Grand Slam*. It had been allocated more time and money than was usual for a programme of this sort and I was intrigued to see that it was listed as being written by the senior script editor and directed by the head of drama. This being most unusual, I decided to investigate and asked for a script. This was a decision I was never to regret for, having decided to allocate the programme to myself, I soon found that I was designing what was to become one of the most popular programmes ever produced by BBC Wales.

John Hefin (Head of Drama), Gwenlyn Parry (Senior Script Editor) and myself were good friends, so working together and sharing ideas came naturally and was a great pleasure. One of the results of these meetings was the decision to spend a few days in Paris, to find locations and to see, among other things, the prison nearest the city, one cell of which I would have to replicate later as a set in Cardiff.

The magical city welcomed us with its well-known landmarks – Notre Dame, and the busy Seine embankments, the open-air cafés with striped umbrellas and the glorious smells of food. An impressive hire-car was laid on for us by the BBC representatives in Paris, of which I was immediately appointed driver as I had been the only one of us who had thought of obtaining an international

The caci-pot.

driving licence. Our first port of call was the prison. While I drove, John and Gwenlyn elected to read the map, which turned out to be a none-too-helpful tourist guide, and not in any way designed to get anyone to the local prison. Fortunately, at precisely the moment that we decided we were irretrievably lost, we saw a police van parked at the side of the road.

To our great relief, on learning that we had an appointment with the governor of the prison, they unexpectedly agreed to provide us with an escort. At extraordinary speeds, they conducted us through the busy streets and, with nerve-racking frequency, guided us through red traffic lights till we got to the Periferique where, if anything, the pace increased even more. My dreams of Formula One were suddenly interrupted by the sight of an angry-looking police motorcyclist in my rear view mirror. John and I tried, with gestures, to convey to him the fact that we were following a police car. We hadn't realised, however, that Gwenlyn's signals to him from the back seat were not of the kind that would get us any help or sympathy. Finally, though, he got the message and with black Gallic looks he sped away, leaving me to catch up with my escort.

We arrived at the gates of the prison, and I will always remember the simulated reluctance of one of the policemen to accept the bottle of duty-free Scotch I offered him, until his partner, grabbing it from my hand, saluted graciously as they sped away laughing.

All these unpredictable adventures had inevitably made us late for our appointment but the coolness we were expecting on arrival was not in evidence. On the contrary, we were entertained with a bottle of wine and a genuine interest in our project. Cameras were strictly off limits, I was told, but with the semblance of a wink the governor chose not to see the Minolta on my shoulder. He did, however, issue a warning not to photograph any of the inmates.

Later that evening, back in the City, one of my friends, a designer with Louis Féraud, agreed to show us around. We were introduced to her luxurious flat, and were most amused when she said she did not have very much to drink but asked apologetically, "Would just champagne do?" She conducted us around a number of places that we were to use later as film locations when we returned. We were shown the Art Nouveau Metro signs, the decorative metal pissoirs and the bars with the ghosts of Daumier, Lautrec and Degas. We savoured the wine and other national drinks in Montmartre with her and, as the evening wore on, sang Piaf's '*La vie en Rose*' and '*Non, je ne regrette rien*', ending inevitably with Welsh hymns, to the enquiring and mystified looks of the locals. It was a useful 'recce', however, and we did get a very good feel for the environment.

Back in Cardiff, we had to decide on where to shoot the various locations required for the film. Fortunately, the old BBC club on Newport Road had an atmosphere that was just about perfect. The right furniture and props of the right colours and of the right period would give the interiors of the old Victorian building the perfect feel. The decorative wooden staircase in the hall was just made for the hotel foyer. The unused rooms upstairs were perfect for the bedrooms, and all the bathroom needed was a hired bidet in the corner. False shutters on the

It's for your downstairs, not your upstairs.

windows would complete the illusion. Downstairs in the cramped basement, we needed a few risqué posters and the imaginative lighting of the cameraman, to create the realistic location for the nightclub, a nightclub that could have held its own with the clubs around the Moulin Rouge. Now, all that was left to design was the prison cell. A few wooden bars, painted as metal, would be enough to imprison the unfortunate Windsor Davies. Judiciously shot, he eventually appeared to the viewer to be safely imprisoned in the cell of the Parisian jail.

Next came the anticipation of returning to Paris, with the cast, to film the exterior scenes. Added to this was the excitement we felt about the results of the forthcoming rugby match, on which the script so much depended. On our arrival, I was once again appointed driver of the hired car, which was also used for filming. I recall having to drive Hugh Griffiths along Haussmann's wonderful wide boulevards and along the banks of the Seine, where one could almost hear the accordions playing. I drove around the Arc de Triomphe, while he stood up in the passenger seat, with his head poking out of the sliding roof, holding an umbrella in his hands to simulate a gun. This would have been difficult enough under normal conditions but, during the Parisian rush hour, it was fraught with danger, especially as there was more than one take, and I knew that permission had not been sought from the police.

We stayed in a very large and popular tourist hotel, surrounded by Japanese holidaymakers with more cameras and camera equipment than we had ourselves. In the interests of economy, everybody was forced to share a room, including even the director and the leading actors, Hugh Griffith and Windsor Davies. There were grumbles, of course there were grumbles, but this was Paris, so no one protested for very long.

Of the whole crew, I turned out to be the most fortunate. The luck of the draw had established as my companion a young man from publicity. It turned out that he had friends in Paris, so he left us to join them and, fortunately, none of us ever saw him again. This had more than one advantage because my room became the centre for late night social meetings and parties. One party in particular stays in my mind because of Gwenlyn's wicked sense of humour. It was our last night in Paris, after a successful shoot, and everyone was in party mode. We had met some German girls in a restaurant earlier and invited them over. As the evening wore on, I noticed that Gwenlyn was regularly leaving the room and returning each time with a card of some kind on which he appeared to write messages. As the whisky became depleted, I thought no more about it and was not really aware of much more till I awoke next morning with a sore head. I carried my bags down to the foyer, to be confronted by what appeared to be an international riot. Hotel staff and guests – Japanese, American, Welsh and English – were all gesticulating and shouting, each in their own language. It took a long time to get to the disgruntled desk clerk to settle our accounts.

Only Gwenlyn was laughing. During our party on the previous night, he had altered all the breakfast cards hanging on the hotel room doors. The Americans had porridge and tea, the Welsh and English had croissants and the Japanese had full English breakfasts!

On the return flight, I collected the autographs of all the actors on the back of a ten franc note, and as an exercise to keep myself occupied, I drew Hugh Griffith and Windsor Davies on the back of a BBC *Grand Slam* script, copies of which I still have today. As I worked, I remembered various other episodes of our stay.

Late one evening, John and I went out for a drive on our own, to get a taste of Paris without the crew and actors. As night approached, it became an enchanted city, the lights transforming it into a fairy-tale playground, where even the sounds and smells miraculously changed. Choosing a street at random, we found ourselves in the world of the 'Ladies of the Night'; choosing another, we were in the world of the élite, surrounded by windows displaying the height of fashion and displays of expensive treats in decorative patisseries. The delicious smells of haute cuisine from countries all over the world reminded me of the Parisian's doctrine: 'A day without a good meal is a day wasted'.

This tempts me to end with the quote: 'A schedule without *Grand Slam* is a schedule wasted!'

Alan Taylor

Mog, Russ, John, and assistant cameraman Ken McKay in Alan's jail.

GET AN EIFFEL

REMEMBER Mog, Maldwyn, Glyn and Caradog who went to Paris to see Wales' 1977 Grand Slam bid? How could you forget – the colourful characters of the hit BBC film Grand Slam won a place in Welsh hearts forever with their macap on-tour antics.

But what would Mog and Co be doing now with the Rugby World Cup on their doorsteps?

MARIA WILLIAMS found out

THE PLOT...

A GROUP of Welsh rugby fans fly to Paris for the 1977 Grand Slam decider in Parc des Prince.

Organised by club Hon Sec Mog Jones, the group's adventures take them to a strip club near the Sacre Coeur after Caradog Lloyd Evans retraces his footsteps as a soldier liberating the city in 1945.

The widower is desperately seeking his "Butterfly", the lithe young woman he bedded at that time but who now turns out to be the club's middle-aged Madame.

Undertaker Caradog is disenchanted, but son Glyn, who is determined to score a different sort of Grand Slam with a willing woman, and Madame's daughter Odette flee when the Welsh lads and French locals get into a fist-fight.

Caradog gives them all a fright when they think he's dead, while impromptu stripper Mog ends up in his vest and pants in jail – and runs to the stadium only to catch the dying seconds and comfort a distraught Maldwyn when the Welsh team loses.

Glyn is so pre-occupied that he forgets the time – and ends up watching the match on TV.

But, as Maldwyn points out in consolation: "It's Cardiff Arms Park, next year."

SPIRIT: Sion Probert now

'Lots of booze – just like a real rugby trip'

SION has worked extensively on stage and radio since Grand Slam but he has never forgotten Maldwyn.

Sion said: "Maldwyn is such a great character. John Hefin, the director of Grand Slam, and I were working on another film when he heard me doing Maldwyn and asked me to do it for Grand Slam. I wrote a lot of the character's lines, and we ad-libbed a great deal.

"Filming Grand Slam was just like going on any rugby trip – lots of booze and a great spirit.

"There was a great story about Hugh Griffith having 13 brandies for breakfast one day during filming. But I had to be in make-up for an hour and half before the others while they sprayed my hair blond and got me into fake fur."

He added: "But what would

SION PROBERT starred as **MALDWYN NOVELLO-PUGHE** – the campest boutique owner in the Valleys

Grunt and Go. And he would have loved the World Cup in Wales."

□WHAT MALDWYN MIGHT SAY TODAY: "Look, I can only spare you a few minutes on the phone, love. These trans-Atlantic calls cost a bleeding fortune, don't they? I'm a bit peeved about the Rugby World Cup actually – those men at the WRU turned down my new strip design for the team. They said fake fur and tight shorts wasn't quite the look they were after. Philistines. I can't get back to watch the matches, because I'm stuck out here with

'It was a poignant moment when they demolished the Arms Park'

WINDSOR DAVIES starred as **MOG JONES**, arguably Wales's finest uncapped rugby player

ANTYMOEL'S Windsor Davies has a soft spot for the character of Mog – unsurprisingly as the role made him a household name in Wales.

The self-confessed rugby fanatic said: "I like Mog immensely.

"But the people who were just like him then have been through so much in the past 22 years.

"Mog was a miner, and now there are no mines. And as for rugby, it has become a professional game.

"I went into Cardiff Arms Park when they were demolishing it and taking out the chairs. I found it a very poignant moment, the idea that this was the end of an era. I'm sure Mog would feel that too. But if Mog was around now, I see

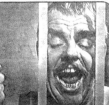

END OF ERA: Windsor Davies

comedy stars, has since taken roles in Vanity Fair and the BBC Wales drama Mortimer's Law.

For the last two months, he's been in

team. And what a team – almost as good as the glory boys Gareth Edwards, JPR and Phil Bennett. That Jenks – what a boot.

OF THIS, MOG!

WINNING TEAM: Sion, Windsor, the late, great Hugh Griffith and Dewi on tour in Grand Slam

Liberated Odette was no prostitute

SHARON MORGAN starred as ODETTE the French beauty who got it together with Glyn Lloyd Evans

SHARON Morgan wants to get one thing straight – the liberated Frenchwoman Odette was not a prostitute.

"One misconception I want to clear up is that Odette was a prostitute. She was not.

KNICKERS ON: Sharon Morgan

"Her mother was the Madame of a brothel, but she was a liberated girl, who saw a bloke she fancied and went to bed with him.

"The whole idea then was that we were being liberated about our sexuality and that women would have sexual equality. It hasn't exactly turned out that way, but Grand Slam was a very innocent film, I think.

She added: "I wasn't completely nude during that bedroom scene, you know. I was wearing knickers. It was done very sensitively, the crew were marvellous, and thankfully, I have a very liberal family. The scene was filmed at the old BBC club on Newport Road in Cardiff, now St Peter's Rugby Club.

"It's difficult to know what Odette would be like now. I like to think of her as well-travelled, having done anything she liked with her life. She was that sort of character. I like the idea that Glyn comes back to look for her. Or perhaps she's already looked for him, married him and now they have eight kids.

Since taking off Odette's glamorous wig, Carmarthen-born Sharon, now 38, worked on the award-winning S4C drama Tair Chwair and BBC Radio Wales's series, Station Road.

She is soon to film another series of A Mind To Kill with Philip Madoc, in which she plays a role a million miles away from the glamorous Odette.

I had to coax Hugh from his sick bed

MARIKA RIVERA starred as MADAME – the mother of Odette

MARIKA Rivera says she saved Grand Slam from being axed by coaxing Hugh Griffith from his sick bed.

Speaking for the first time about Grand Slam, she said: "Hugh was very ill in hospital, and I went to visit him.

SAVIOUR: Marika Rivera

"The director told me he feared Hugh would die before the film was completed, so he sent me into the ward to try and tease him back to life.

"I said: 'I've never worked with the famous Hugh Griffith before. Let's finish the film. Let me be your Butterfly. You can die afterwards.'

"Gradually, his eyes began to open, and we went off and did the film."

She added: "I remember Sharon as being a very beautiful girl, and we all got on very well, like a big family.

"Hugh Griffith said he didn't like French women, but I told him that I was really Mexican/Russian, and so we got on from there. It was such fun to work on that film, and afterwards, it made me quite a star in Wales."

No plans for Slam sequel

SO, will there ever be a sequel? Not according to its writer and director John Hefin.

John, who lives in Borth, near Aberystwyth, said: "I have never been tempted to make a sequel, because I always felt that it would be like having something which had been warmed up. But I do dream about the characters and what they would be like now.

Hefin, who co-wrote Grand Slam with the late Gwenlyn Parry, said: "These days, Mog would be organising the travel for the Welsh team in the World Cup – and sending them to the wrong venues.

DREAMS: John Hefin

"I think Glyn would have repeated the life of his father and taken over the family business. I reckon Maldwyn would be the first gay First Secretary of Wales. I bet Madame would have

Hugh had a case like a cocktail cabinet...

NERVES: Dewi Morris

DEWI Morris's mum stopped going to chapel after she saw her son in risqué scenes in Grand Slam.

Swansea-born Dewi, 51, said: "It was near the knuckle for those days. I remember that my mother refused to go to chapel when she first saw it because she was so embarrassed.

"The deacon and the minister came to visit her and find out if she was ill, or something, and they said: 'We loved that new film Glyn is in.'

"So she started going again. But now, she tells everyone that her son was in Grand Slam. She's proud of it."

He added: "I remember the first day of filming, Hugh Griffith saw I was nervous and beckoned me over. I went thinking he wanted to discuss the script.

"Instead, he opened up a case he carried with him, and inside it was a complete cocktail cabinet. Then he offered me a drink.

DEWI MORRIS starred as GLYN LLOYD EVANS – one of the two cheery undertakers on tour with his dad, Caradog, who was played by the late Hugh Griffith

undertaker, and would perhaps go in search of Odette. "It would be funny to think that the two might continue the story by falling in love. He'd be really excited about the World Cup – and be at every match."

□ **WHAT GLYN MIGHT SAY TODAY:** "I'm divorced now, so I'll get to see as many of the matches as I like without the wife getting in the way. I've never recovered from missing the Grand Slam match – even if I've got some fond memories instead. Duw, she was a hell of a girl. I've got my World Cup

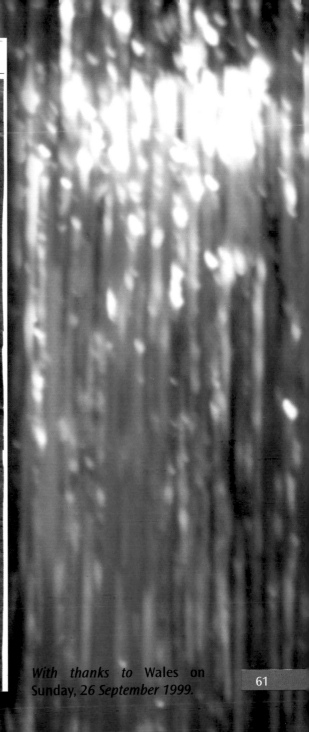

With thanks to Wales on Sunday, *26 September 1999.*

Windsor Davies

Mog Jones

A welcome coffee – mid-stripping to 'Egyptian Reggae'.

My occupation has given me great pleasure most of the time. *Grand Slam* was probably the most enjoyable. Memory tends to play tricks, which is to say that I cannot swear to complete accuracy in these recollections, but they are definitely extremely happy.

Some signposts that stand out:

Walking in an informal group up the stairs at Rhoose airport;

Talking to one of our heroes, Mervyn Davies; this was already getting a bit rich for the blood;

Marika playing her part to perfection as the nightclub proprietress, see John Betjeman's poem, 'Sun and Fun';

Siôn Probert's story of the newly widowed woman talking to a sympathetic neighbour, "He'd only just gone out to get a cabbage from the garden."

"Oh, there's terrible. What did you do?"
"I opened a tin of peas instead."

It is a truth universally acknowledged that actors belong to a mutual admiration society, at least in public. However, this is subjective and because I have

such fond memories of this time I can truthfully say that I think the whole company was brilliant, all the way down to John Hefin. I hope Patagonians have a sense of humour. [My grandfather was born in a cave in Puerto Madryn, Patagonia! – Ed.]

The ground floor of the Hotel du Nord in Paris seemed vast, in retrospect at least. It was packed with Welsh fans full of brotherly love and Brain's SA, the Welsh beer fondly known as Skull Attack. There was a major hiccup in the proceedings as word went round that stocks of SA had dried up. It was true and we were being offered something called Stella Artois. Our grudging response was considerably lightened when the next word that went round was in the nature of, "Hey, it's not bad, this stuff, is it?"

So, on with the motley. Should readers get the impression that this was just some carefree pre-match Mardi Gras they would be exactly right. The serious stuff would occur the next day. The point I am making is that dotted here and there in this lively crowd was a team of highly disciplined actors, led by the great Hugh Griffith, to name but a few, poised to file out when called to film in the streets of Paris.

OK. Cut to Saturday morning. The film called for me to jog, pace and walk through Paris in a red vest and rather brief shorts. It had to be a determined effort on my part to avoid the attentions of the curious, Welsh or French, who might be tempted to stop and chat or whatever,

'Who had to share a bed with Maldwyn?
Muggins Mog.'

and then to approach the stadium, in those days the Parc des Princes. We were filming earlyish, so as yet there was only a scattering of fans about, but there was a very large crowd of police, business-like and bristling with side arms and not a few sub-machine guns. Simultaneously, I recalled a mention that the President of France would be attending the match. I remember thinking that one of those coppers just might have a seizure and mow me down, or maybe JH would have a seizure and be unable to say, "Cut."

The club scene was wild, of course, and there was our lovely Hugh struggling to rekindle his lost youth. Dewi had his own agenda with the daughter, and Moc and the boys were just enjoying the performance of the striptease artiste.

Now, cut live to Nantymoel, near Bridgend, for real. My mother was watching aghast – how would she make her way to Bethel chapel after that? In the event, two ladies of the church, a very jolly pair, who always seemed to be laughing anyway, spluttered their delight to my mother, saying that it was, "Great," and, "It's lovely to have a good laugh at the television for a change."

Windsor Davies

Twenty minutes to kick-off.

If anybody knew Paris by night, it was Marika, and just before joining us on Grand Slam, *she had been directed by Federico Fellini in* Casanova; *follow that!*

Sharon Morgan

Odette

"The archetypal French woman, complete with gorgeous, silky, Purdey-style wig, loads of black eyeliner, and lip gloss."

I've always felt an affinity with France; one of my earliest childhood memories is of my mother singing 'Frère Jacques' and 'Au Claire de la Lune' to me in my bath. I'd discovered the Eiffel Tower and 'Orangina' on the school trip, and I had a sultry French pen pal; she visited me in Llandyfaelog, and she picked some foxgloves and fell for the charms of a certain Jeff Diamond. I visited her in Pont L'Eveque, in Normandy, where I drove through cherry-blossomed orchards and ate horse and tripe. I knew all the words to every Françoise Hardy song I could lay my hands on. And I only chose History instead of French at university because I couldn't bear the thought of doing Latin A level.

But it certainly never occurred to me that one day I'd be standing freezing in my knickers, somewhere in the depths of the BBC, being painted all over with pancake make-up by the wonderfully witty Cissian Rees, make-up artist extraordinaire, as the preliminary part of my transformation into Odette – the archetypal French woman, complete with gorgeous, silky, Purdey-style wig, loads of black eyeliner, and lip gloss. So many agents and casting directors were to be disappointed when I walked into auditions, all blonde curls and fair skin.

When John offered me the part, I leapt at it,

le "moment of truth".

nudity or no nudity, and I am still amazed at the faith he had in me.

I brushed up my French accent in English, with the help of Patrick, who lived on the Taff embankment, did a lot of vigorous exercises and was only vaguely comforted when Colleen O'Brien, the brilliant costume designer, assured me that it was perfectly normal for French women's stomachs to stick out a bit.

We shopped for Odette at the Red Barn, an antique and vintage clothes shop in Pontcanna. The shirt I wore has long gone, but I still have the beautiful black and pink net scarf. It brings me luck; I was wearing it when I won my Bafta for Best Actress in 1998.

Of course, I never got to Paris. All my filming took place in the old BBC club in Newport Road, a building whose bar I was already familiar with. There was a script and we rehearsed, but a lot of it was ad-libbed, particularly, in my case, in the scene where Glyn and Odette watch the match in bed, accompanied by many cigarettes and several glasses of wine, hence the slight softening noticeable around my eyes.

Oh, the ease of it and the pleasure of it all! I had worked with John before; he'd cast me on my first ever television job, *Rhandir Mwyn* (a thirteen-part drama about the Quakers in America), and I'd also acted with Dewi many times, including the first ever Welsh language Welsh pantomime, *Mawredd Mawr*. I'd also worked with Cissian and Colleen on *Pobol y Cwm* and very soon got to know and trust Russ, the cameraman, and Mansel on sound.

Trust is a pretty necessary component of the relationship between director, actors and crew, and such was the nature of the business in those days that we took it all for granted.

As for the nudity and the sex, it didn't worry me, although it did worry my then boyfriend as we walked around Llyn Cwellyn, arguing. I did want to look beautiful and sexy and desirable, of course. It's

strange how all that painful 27-year-old anxiety about body image fades away as I watch the film now, 30 years on. But far more important for me, as with any acting job, was creating a believable character. I wanted Odette to be convincingly French, but not just French, but that woman, in that place, experiencing those particular emotions.

For me, Odette was a free spirit who, if she wanted to make love to someone, would, with no strings attached, for the pure joy of it. For this was in the 70s, before Thatcherism arrived, with its peculiar form of repression and its universal commoditisation, and I believe that we women were on our way to equality and sexual liberation in a world where there would be no double standards and where women would no longer be sluts and whores, when men were studs and a 'bit of a boy'. And I dream on!

Grand Slam happened in a busy time in my career. I was juggling another two or three jobs at the same time. *Grand Slam* was just another one of those jobs, albeit a wonderful one. By the time it was broadcast in '77, I was appearing in *Under Milk Wood* in the Mayfair Theatre, and had moved to London; and so I was completely unaware of the public reaction in Wales. I had no idea that it had practically achieved iconic status overnight, and it is quite an achievement to have held onto that, 30 years on.

Romantic, innocent and gloriously funny, *Grand Slam* portrays intense moments in the characters' lives, ephemeral by definition. Acting is an ephemeral business and it's a wonderful feeling to have been part of something that has stood the test of time.

Sharon Morgan

Odette has just seen Glyn's stand ticket.

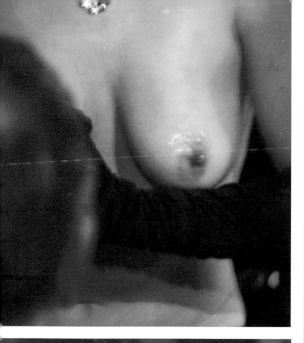

Martin Griffiths' specs are put to the test. (Martin was one of the kindest men, who sadly is not with us any more.)

Siôn Probert

Maldwyn Novello-Pughe

'*When I do go, I do go!*'

What can I say about *Grand Slam* that hasn't already been said?

For me, it was a most joyous experience: I'm happy and flattered to be able to write that, to this day, people still request autographs and ask me to quote 'M's' lines (few of which I remember accurately, as much of the script was ad-libbed as we proceeded with this romp).

No actor could wish for a better cast with whom to work; we enjoyed one another's company and input enormously and I'm still in touch with Windsor, Dewi, Sharon and my great friend Elizabeth Morgan who played the hotel receptionist: she and I have appeared in all aspects of theatre, radio and televison for longer than I care to remember, and have written many scripts together.

Sharon and I played in the West End for almost a year in *Under Milk Wood* and subsequently as husband and wife in *The Citadel* for BBC television. I had worked with Windsor prior to *Grand Slam*, and also with Hugh Griffiths's sister,

Elen Roger Jones, who was a delight.

The supporting artists must be mentioned, all of whom joined into the spirit of the production wholeheartedly, in particular Kim Karlisle, the exotic dancer, and Dai Davies, World Gurning Champion.

My contribution to the film was a total fluke; a film that has been described as 'The Icon of Welsh comedy'.

John Hefin was directing a most moving film by Rhydderch Jones entitled *Mr Lollipop M.A.* with Dame Flora Robson and Charles Williams, in which I played a social worker.

During filming, usually over a pint (or six) I happened to tell John a couple of jokes which he found very funny. Shortly afterwards, having repeated the jokes to Gwenlyn Parry (who had initiated *Grand Slam* in a very different format in the Welsh language), it was decided that Maldwyn Novello-Pughe should be featured in the film.

Having played mainly serious roles in my varied work, I leapt at the opportunity, hoping with some fear and trepidation that I could do justice to such an outlandish character.

My main concern was that I would have to make him sufficiently 'acceptable to the boys' for them to even consider allowing him to join them on the Paris trip. Thanks to the reactions of the cast, whose general attitude was 'Take no notice of 'im, it's only Maldwyn'. (Who after all 'only wanted to see the shops'.) To my great relief, it worked.

I had no idea with whom I would be working when M was taken into the fold. Later John, Dewi and I met up and there was an immediate rapport between Dewi and myself; we are friends to this day (as is his wife Rhiannon) despite his grabbing me by my balls unexpectedly in one scene: 'Wait till you're asked, will you?' was M's dismissive yet eager response.

M has told me strictly privately that he'd love Dewi to do it again – but not so hard next time'.

As for the crew – Russ on an innovative hand-held camera (pretty rare in those days); Mansel "We can't do it, John," 'Sound' Davies; John's P.A. Beth; Colleen 'Costume' O' Brien, and Cissian Rees who did our Make up… thereby hangs a tale, but I'm sworn to secrecy unless Cissian offers me a large bribe in order to protect her reputation!!

As I recall, the 'Powers that Were' at the BBC decreed that *Grand Slam* should be truncated

'Wait till you're asked, will you!'

by 30 minutes in order to accommodate another programme in BBC 1's schedule – a programme which has disappeared into the mists of time, unlike *Grand Slam*. Shame on them.

Among the footage lost to us was a brilliant improvisation by Dillwyn Owen who played the permanently drunk Will Posh.

Prior to his hilarious dropping of the cans of Felinfoel bitter on the stairs at Rhoose airport (which is included) Dillwyn invented a brilliant scene on the coach; a scenario concerning his wife and the committee, (whatever that was) which lasted several minutes. It was a classic.

I did my very first radio job with Dillwyn when I was eleven years old. Who could have wished for a better 'feed' than he? In one of the final takes (to all intents and purposes at Parc des Princes but in actual

Wicked!

fact Cardiff Arms Park), the 'Yew dribble down my fun fur one more time and I'll snap yewer beads for yew!' scene, his character was so 'off his head' he never responded coherently to anything that was said to him. It was immaterial what M was babbling on about although we both 'corpsed rotten' once John had shouted 'cut' at the end of the take.

There are many examples of scenes such as this that enhanced our output. Among them I would have to cite the one in the aeroplane with Huw involving 'Two buckles and no end'. At the beginning I had asked Huw whether he'd mind my improvising with him. He generously agreed, adding 'You can throw anything at me boy, and I'll just roll my eyes... how the hell do you think I won an Oscar?' He almost 'went', though, with the unexpected 'Two buckles and no end' line – as did I. (I'd never intended to get the straps on the seat belts mixed up. I had never flown before!)

Green with envy over the prowess of his cast, John decided to grab his own few seconds of fame by emerging from a pissoir in Montmartre shaking his leg as he left (rumour has it that he was readjusting his panty hose), emulating Alfred Hitchcock, who appears briefly in all his own films. Watch carefully next time and you'll clock it. (Those of a nervous disposition should turn to another channel.) To my regret I never again worked with John, basically because he didn't ask me – THE SWINE.

I must give due credit to our brilliant editor Chris Lawrence (a Bafta award winner) for inserting (don't break out into a sweat now, Chris) the 'Novello' into Maldwyn's name. My contribution was to add the 'e' into Pughe. Well, Maldwyn does revel in affectation, to say the least!

I have enjoyed all my work over the years – in theatre, RSC and ESC; many other television plays and hundreds of radio broadcasts; but *Grand Slam* will always evoke the fondest of memories not only for the challenge with which it presented me, but to know that our Great Welsh Nation has taken the film to its warm heart.

I'm just grateful that it was greeted everywhere with the success it deserved. What a holiday! What a job! What fun!

Diolch yn fawr iawn i bawb!

Siôn Probert

Beth Price
Production Assistant

The first night in Paris augured so well. Amazingly, we'd landed safely at Charles de Gaulle Airport, on schedule at 5.20pm, filming en route. We had kept shooting as we were landing – so incredibly tight was our filming schedule; so much for health and safety! We continued filming through customs, passport control and all the way to the Hôtel Terminus in Gare du Nord.

"And that's enough," said John, to total agreement from the crew and cast. "Let's go for a meal," we all said, "and meet at reception in half an hour."

I went up in a crowded lift, full of Welshmen who spoke Welsh (not a Welsh woman in sight). They made various comments about me, all very nice but all a bit 'Rugby after ten pints' (you know what I mean, girls?). I recognised their accent as it was the accent of my childhood, so as I was leaving the lift and just as the doors were closing, I turned and said, "*Cofiwch fi at Gwmgiedd, bois!*" (Remember me to Cwmgiedd, boys!) I'll always remember their shocked faces.

We all shared rooms. I had tried every which way to get better accommodation, but Paris was full, and our budget didn't allow for posh hotels. Hugh shared with Windsor (not a sign of any prima donna Hollywood Oscar winner behaviour in sight!), Dewi with Siôn, John with Gwenlyn, and so it went on. No one grumbled or complained: we were a whinge-free zone.

Reception saw us all washed and scrubbed (some more than others) and off to go in various taxis to Les Argonalites, 12 Rue de la Huchette, a lovely, ordinary restaurant on the Left Bank, not very far from Shakespeare & Co. (one of the great bookshops of the world).

We arrived more or less on time, and the usual muddle of mass ordering began. Eventually, we all got tucked in, the wine flowed and then, inevitably, some of our company began to sing; softly at first, but building, with the intake of wine, to a crescendo. The maître d' came over and asked us to stop singing – which we did, fair play to our host country (that we were going to hammer tomorrow, as Mog would have it). But then the rest of the restaurant diners said, "No, no, let them sing!" which we did, and then they sang too, and before the next bottle of house rouge was downed, we had an Eisteddfod. There were no prizes except pleasure!

As we sat in a circle I could see the faces of my friends; John and Gwenlyn were, as usual, deep in conversation, punctuated with the usual loud laughter. So much rested on their shoulders. My small problem was to keep track of the script every day, as part of my job included logging every word of dialogue with exact timings of every scene – not easy with this mercurial lot, who changed/invented everything as we went along. It was a challenge, but it was a happy one.

Then, I looked around and saw Hugh enjoying his Armagnac, with the rest of the cast and crew gathered around his Falstaffian figure, relishing his outrageous recollections. Amongst other things, he was recounting shooting the opening hearse scene, back in the Rhondda. Winding their way down valley roads, Hugh and Dewi could see strange cars

Gren's gift to Beth.

join the cortège thinking they were following a bona fide family coffin. The poor dabs' response, as the truth dawned on them, was, that night in Paris, hilarious.

Little did I realise that evening that I would shortly be accompanying him and a nurse back from Paris to Rhoose, and straight to the Heath Hospital. *Grand Slam* was to be his last film.

On that lovely evening in Paris, we were all oblivious of his fate. For all that we knew, all that was certain as far as tomorrow's schedule was concerned, was that at 2.30 we'd film Wales playing France at the Parc des Princes, and of course, Wales would win. How little we knew.

Beth Price

And so – to the final contributor, to the book and the film. His immense, immeasurable contribution to the latter was in so many ways the key to its success – "a guy called Chris" (see Ode, p84).

Chris Lawrence
Chef du Montage

Chris wearing Peter O'Toole's hat – but that's another story.

After nearly 45 years as a film editor, I can remember most of the films I've edited. Some are best forgotten, but others stay firmly in my mind. After 30 years, I remember many of the joys of working on *Grand Slam* and many of the challenges of putting it all together.

These days, I rarely go out on location, mainly because there is so little time, and, more importantly, because I want to retain my objectivity; if an editor is aware of all the various problems during the shoot, his or her choice of material may be influenced during the cutting process. Every shot should be in the film because it works in the context of the whole film, and not because it took three days to shoot, or two men were injured when the set fell over. On *Grand Slam,* however, I did go for one day, when they were filming scenes in the Paris hotel, the hotel foyer and the bedroom scenes. It was not a long journey because the location was the BBC club in Newport Road, Cardiff – some of *Grand Slam* was filmed in Paris, but the vast majority was filmed in Cardiff.

Watching the rushes was exciting. Some scenes were scripted, but most were improvised by the actors (briefed by the director, John Hefin). As with any film shot in that way, we had far more material than we would need to make a 75-minute film. The eventual ratio was about 12 to 1.

To make a sequence on film is quite a long process – unlike today, working on a computer, when an editor can have several versions of a sequence in minutes. In those days, making changes in a film sequence meant taking apart the joins and hanging the celluloid shots in the trim bin, and starting again. To lengthen the shot, the assistant editor would have to find the trim and rejoin it to the main shot ("Complicated beyond," as Maldwyn would say). Eventually, of course, the sequence came together.

One of the main problems in making a film is the cutting rhythm, and the very first sequence can influence the whole balance of the film.

Establishing the main characters and getting them on their way was fairly straightforward. It was at the airport that the real editing began. We had good footage of the actors and the Welsh rugby team, all about to board the planes to Paris, which was fine.

Our plane journey had some scripted lines but was mostly improvised (e.g. the classic 'Two buckles and no end'). Likewise, the taxi sequence to Paris was all set up, but most of the dialogue was again improvised. The actors had developed a wonderful relationship and sparked off each other brilliantly.

For me, the most exciting part of *Grand Slam* was the rugby match itself. We had so many elements to work with:

- Real footage of the match, filmed by Russ from the touch line in Paris
- French television coverage of the game
- Mog watching the game on TV in prison
- Glyn watching TV in Odette's bedroom
- Footage of Welsh and French fans arriving at the stadium and watching the game
- The Dax band playing before the game
- Our actors arriving and watching the game, including Maldwyn worrying

We had several stories to develop. Would Glyn see a Grand Slam? Mog was in jail – would he get to the game? Would the Welsh team achieve a Grand Slam and would Maldwyn stop worrying?

John and Gwenlyn had scripted the match day, but because so much of the material was 'actuality footage', filmed by the brilliant cameraman Russ Walker, we realised very early on that this would be a sequence that would need much more work and plotting than any script could provide. Every story had to be told and woven together so as to create an accessible story line, with tension and excitement. We decided to use a huge white card, and list all the elements on it, using a pencil, which meant we could erase and alter any sequence as we went along. We worked out an order and I assembled a sequence. It took me some time, and we watched it through excitedly. It wasn't working. It was too long, the order was confusing and it lacked excitement. We went back to our very large card. John and I stood in front of it and talked the sequence through again and again. We changed the order and stood back and changed it yet again! Unlike today's computer editing, where every version can be retained and watched over and over; every time we decided to

Will Posh, for once, is lost for words.

make changes we lost the latest version as I'd taken it apart to reassemble it. Finally, finally, I assembled the new order and we reviewed the re-cut. It had taken several days to complete the sequence and insert it into the body of the film, and although, 30 years on, I would possibly tweak one or two orders and lengths, I think the sequence in the finished film was not too bad.

Another complicated sequence to edit was the Strip Club, not so much the picture, but the sound. If the sound is not right – in the blend of speech effects and music – the film is difficult to watch and the audience gets bored. In the Strip Club, we had the pictures, the music, and the dialogue involving Maldwyn telling the 'Tesco' joke, urging Mog to go the 'whole hog', fancying Charles Aznevour and the resultant fight.

When the sequence was finished, it almost worked but the sound was 'lumpy'. We needed something to pull it all together, such as crowd noises, shouts and cheers. We searched and searched but all the sound effects we found were too short and lacked any real feeling of raucous Welsh rugby fans who might possibly visit a Strip Club.

The dubbing mixer, Tony Heaseman, and I devised an answer. In the BBC film unit, there was a lot of interest from other editing staff, eager to see the rugby footage. The door of our small editing room in Newport Road had been kept firmly shut during the editing, jealously guarding our material. However, we invited members of the unit to a sort of 'Premiere'.

This would be the first time the strip club sequence, or any part of the film, was to be shown to those not working on it. Tony had rigged hidden microphones in the dubbing theatre, to record the sound we needed – not a normal practice. As we ran the sequence on screen, Tony recorded our colleagues' excellent if predictable reactions. Mixed with the music and dialogue, the sound worked at last.

Of course, the choice of music was all important. John wanted 'Plaisir d'Amour' to represent Mr Lloyd-Evans' memories of wartime Paris, and we used three different versions of the tune in the film. 'Black Betty' seemed perfect for the stripper (although we had to replace it, for copyright reasons, when the film was sold to Australia and Norway). 'Egyptian Reggae' could have been written for Mog's strip in the club, the Beatles accompanied the second stripper, whilst the Motors track in the Metro scene provided the theme for Mr Lloyd-Evans' search for the Bistro Paradis. Eventually, we finished Grand Slam with a length of 75 minutes – almost feature-film length.

Three or four days before transmission, like a bolt out of the blue, we received a message from London, requesting that, because of industrial action, the film would need to end before midnight, when the plugs would be pulled. Our transmission started at 11pm, so we had to lose 15 minutes: a fifth of the film; an enormous cut.

One or two hotel scenes could go quite easily and we'd have lost seven minutes. With a sick feeling in our stomachs, we trawled desperately for other cuts.

Whilst working, even during a coffee break, Russ had filmed the most beautiful shot in slow motion of two young French people kissing in a café. This was Maldwyn's romantic Paris, and we'd made a sequence showing him in total bliss as he glimpsed the Paris of his dreams. However, something had to go, and as Maldwyn's sequence was pure reverie, John and I reluctantly realised that cutting it was the only answer to a prickly problem. We hit the new 60-minute slot by seconds and we made the BBC 1 transmission on time. However, I felt that the Maldwyn sequence had given a balance to the whole film – which I still miss today.

Working on *Grand Slam* with John taught me

lessons I've never forgotten. It taught me to allow for the unexpected – unscripted rushes, actors improvising, brilliant cameramen getting the most delightful material … and BBC staff going on strike. *Grand Slam* was '*un travail d'amour*'!

John, I know, kept the big white card that had been so useful during the weeks of cutting. One of my fondest souvenirs of *Grand Slam*, amongst many, is a letter from Maldwyn, asking me to call and see him at the boutique and offering me a special discount. I never went; always too busy with the next film and its own particular challenge.

Chris Lawrence

The Press invite to the Preview (designed by Keith Trodden). That Preview was a real test of nerves.

The Ode

Prior to Chris's editing, the dub, the preview, and the transmission, was the end–of–shoot party – when this ode was sung by the cast – an ode which more or less says it all!

Originally performed at the 'Parabie Rue du port nouveau. CAERDYDD
ORCHESTRATION: BY DEWI MORRIS.
CHOREOGRAPHY: BY SIÔN (TO KNOW HIM IS TO LOVE HIM) PROBERT.
VOCALS: BY WINDSOR (GET THE COAL IN, MAM) DAVIES.

"ODE TO BIG JOHN"

Every day at Llandaff you could see him arrive,

He was six foot two, and weighed six forty-five:

Kinda narrow at the shoulder, and broad at the hip,

And everybody knew they could give a lot of stick

To Big John,

Big John

Two-Shot John.

Now John met this dude called Gwenlyn Parry,

A cross between 'Sooty' and 'Dirty Harry',

He was hard and mean and his hair was grey,

But could he write a script?....NO WAY!

Not Gwen

Gwenlyn

Gay Parree,

Well Gwen wrote this play by the name of 'Grand Slam'

So John went ahead wuth his 'two-shots' and 'pan'.

With Russ on the camera, and Mansel on sound

You should have seen the way that they messed around

With 'Grand Slam',

'Grand Slam'
Ond paham?
Bhāhahanh

Now the editor was a guy named Chris

And when he saw the rushes he went straight on the piss,

As he ran from B.H. he was heard to say:

"Thank Gdd for the actors - they've saved the day

For Big John

Big Jo-ohn

NOT ON!"

(Tha author would like to say that any

resemblance to person, or persons living or dead is
entirely coincidental ~ and he hopes that the 'royalties'
will enable him to buy a new typewriter'.)

Postscript

There was only one major decision to take when I was invited to edit this book – and that was to ask the experts on *Grand Slam* to contribute. Some said as a reaction to that decision, 'Oh, cameramen can't write; like editors, they're visual, not verbal'. How wrong they were. Every which one of the cast and crew sent me gems and it was therefore a delight to edit their recollections.

Many of my own memories were rekindled and enriched. Some of their recollections confirmed my own, others didn't, and I found that interesting; after all, we all have individual takes on events – especially with the hindsight of thirty years. I've therefore kept what seems at first sight to be repetition, or conflicting testimony, as I believe a subjective, multifaceted recall makes for a more readable, possibly more accurate, diary of those events long ago.

The pictures were all taken at the time of the shoot and somehow survived in a box in the attic. Alan Taylor took most of them, and as well as being a valuable record, they are in every sense 'happy snaps'; it goes without saying that without them the book would be the poorer.

As for the future; rumour has it that there's to be a sequel. Where do these rumours start! The answer is Bryn Roberts – another extraordinary enabler, from Barcud Derwen (the biggest post-production company outside London). Based on a screenplay that seems to be acceptable to the movers and shakers, Bryn has been actively pursuing both facilities and hard cash to make the sequel (titled *Au Revoir*), a reality.

In the meantime, there remains one most pleasant privilege – no duty, this – which is to say '*diolch yn fawr*' to Gwenlyn, without whom... and to Ray, true and brave friend. Gerald... genius, who was there. The superb cast and crew... of course. The BBC, for their kind co-operation... as always. The *Western Mail* and *Wales on Sunday* for the cuttings. Y Lolfa... to Lefi (my first and probably my last commissioning Editor), and Dafydd – *dyluniwr da*, and finally, Elin – who has not only made sense of my scribbling, but who's also an inspiration as well as my severest critic.

Au Revoir!

J.H.

P.P.S. And now for the afficionados, please turn to the next page.

J.

Quiz

1. What was Auntie Gwennie's husband's name?

2. Where did Auntie Gwennie shop? A) Lidl B)Tesco or C) the Co-op?

3. What was the final score of our unusual defeat in Paris?

4. Who was the Welsh captain?

5. Finish the following quotes:
   'I've got two ……… and no ……… !'

6. 'It's not every day you have a ……… like that'

7. 'If you dribble once more over my ……… '

8. Glyn was described as 'Llwynhendy's answer to ……… ?

9. What was 'Bigger than I thought, mind'?

10. What was Mog's wife called?

11. What is Parc des Princes now?

12. Who broke a shoulder bone in the game?

13. 'A widow's bed is a ……… bed'

14. 'I'll be up that boulevard like a ……… '

15. Which beer did Wil Posh drop in Rhoose Airport?

16. What was described as being 'For your downstairs, not your upstairs'?

17. Who said 'I'll have you in ashes'?

18. Whose roots could you see from the terraces?

19. What did Glyn do to prompt the line 'Wait till you're asked'?

20. On what days does Maldwyn's boutique open late?

21. Which perfume did Mog Jones buy for his wife from duty free?

22. What was the name of the trip's travel agent?

23. What was the name of the pilot of the plane? 'Captain ……… '

24. Which aircraft did they see out of the plane window at Charles de Gaulle?

25. What was the title of the theme music?

26. What was the name of the artist who drew the cartoons for the opening and closing sequence?

27. What did Mog call his jailer?

28. Who played the part of 'My little Butterfly'?

29. What music did Mog strip to in the strip club?

30. Where did Mog buy his boxer shorts?

31. What is the first line of the film?

32. What was Mr Lloyd-Evans's wife called?

33. Which university scarf did Glyn wear?

34. Which drinks did Mr Lloyd-Evans order for himself and Maldwyn on the plane?

35. What union did Glyn and Caradog Lloyd-Evans belong to?

36. What was Charles Aznavour's reaction to Madwyn?

37. What did Mog do when Phil Bennet's abilities were questioned by a Frenchman?

38. Name one graffiti on the wall of the gaol?

39. Name two things that Maldwyn carried onto the plane?

40. Which position should Mog have played for Wales, according to Glyn?

41. What did Mr Lloyd-Evans call the strippers?

42. Name the Metro station that Mr Lloyd-Evans and Maldwyn exit from.

43. Who said – 'I'd take that to the specialist, Doctor!'

44. What was the full name of the travel agent who organised the trip?

45. What was the name of the strip club?

46. Name the Welsh folk song that Mog sang in front of the mirror whilst preparing to go out on the town.

47. What, according to Glyn and Maldwyn, was 'rampant on the continent'?

48. Which autographs had Maldwyn already got on his ball?

49. Which club did Mog play for in the 50s?

50. Which wine did Wil Posh dislike?

ANSWERS ON NEXT PAGE

but be warned:

0–10 'Opeless

10–30 Tidy

30–45 Very tidy

45–49 Crackin'

50/50-Epic! You are definitely the next Wales coach!!!

Quiz Answers

1. Denzil

2. Tesco

3. 16–9 to the French

4. Phil Bennett

5. 'Buckles' and 'end'

6. 'Weekend'

7. 'Fun fur'

8. Sacha Distel

9. Eiffel Tower

10. Morwenna

11. A soccer pitch

12. Gerald Davies

13. 'Cold, cold bed'

14. 'A bat out of hell'

15. Felinfoel

16. The bidet

17. Mr Caradog Lloyd-Evans

18. Jean-Pierre Reive

19. He grabbed Maldwyn's 'down belows'

20. Tuesdays and Thursdays

21. Madam Rochas

22. Happy Valley International

23. Captain Baston

24. Concorde

25. *Plaisir d'Amour*

26. Gren

27. 'French caci-pot'

28. Marika Rivera

29. *Egyptian Reggae*

30. Maldwyn's Boutique

31. Glyn 'I knew you couldn't stand the pace see'

32. Jane

33. Aberystwyth

34. Half a dozen brandy minatures and a Babycham

35 The National Union of Undertakers

36. 'Do us a favour'

37. Windsor pours half a pint over him

38. 'Keith Rowlands wos here'

39. A Teddy bear and a new rugby ball

40. Hooker

41. The Whores of Moab

42. Metropolitan

43. Mog Jones

44. Dedwydd Burke

45. Bistro Paradis

46. *Bugeilio'r Gwenith Gwyn*

47. Rabies

48. Geoff Wheel and JPR

49. Llanelli

50. Chateau Neuf du Crap

Kim Karlisle, the Exotic Dancer, has removed Martin's specs, and is subjecting them to even further tests.

Also available on DVD
Grand Slam: the feature film
www.dukevideo.com
Tel: 01624 640000

£14.99
GUDVD6148

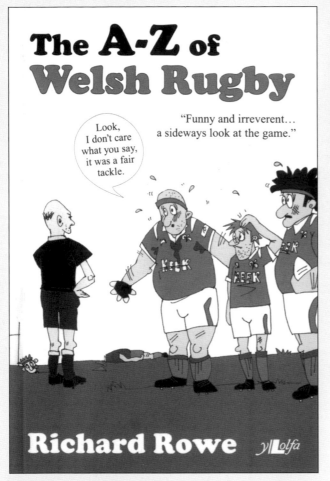

Tales of drunkenness abound in this remarkable field study. Sordid stories of going-away trips with behind-the-scenes insights.

£3.95

ISBN: 0 86243 948 5

Here for the first time the stories from the 'away trips' are published, for the wives to know what it's all about.

£3.95

ISBN: 0 86243 871 3

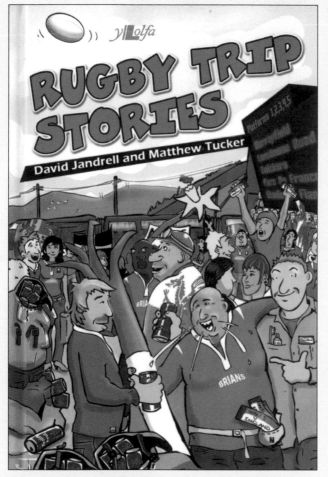

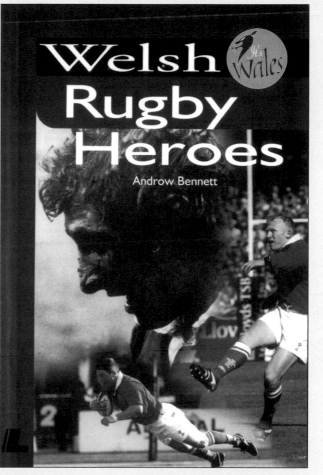

The unsavoury exploits, jokes and drinking stories from rugby trips in the best tournament in the world.

£3.95

ISBN: 0 86243 871 5

A fascinating illustrated book offering an entertaining introduction to various Welsh rugby heroes of the 20th century.

£3.95

ISBN: 0 86243 552 3

Grand Slam is just one of a whole range
of publications from Y Lolfa. For a full
list of books currently in print, send now
for your free copy of our new full-colour
catalogue. Or simply surf into our website

www.ylolfa.com

for secure on-line ordering.

y Lolfa

TALYBONT CEREDIGION CYMRU SY24 5AP
e-mail ylolfa@ylolfa.com
website www.ylolfa.com
phone (01970) 832 304
fax 832 782